SUPER-
POWER
GOLF

SUPER-POWER GOLF

DR. GARY WIREN, **PGA** PROFESSIONAL
WITH DAWSON TAYLOR

Contemporary Books, Inc.
Chicago

Library of Congress Cataloging in Publication Data

Wiren, Gary.
   Super-power golf.

   Includes index.
   1. Golf.   2. Swing (Golf)   3. Golf—Drive.   I. Taylor,
Dawson.   II. Title.
GV965.W73   1984   796.352'3   84-5025
ISBN 0-8092-5465-4

Published by Contemporary Books, Inc.
180 North Michigan Avenue, Chicago, Illinois 60601
Manufactured in the United States of America
Library of Congress Catalog Card Number: 84-5025
International Standard Book Number: 0-8092-5465-4

Published simultaneously in Canada by Beaverbooks, Ltd.
195 Allstate Parkway, Valleywood Business Park
Markham, Ontario L3R 4T8 Canada

TO IONE, FOR HER PATIENCE,
UNDERSTANDING, AND
CONSTANT ENCOURAGEMENT
—*GW*

TO THE "FAMILY FOURSOME."
—*DT*

CONTENTS

FOREWORD

Without special physical conditioning, I could never have competed as successfully as I have in my career. This becomes particularly true now as I approach senior status. Personally, I enjoy working out. For those who haven't experienced the joy of being in condition, I'd strongly recommend it for a happier life, not to mention for better golf.

I've been with thousands of amateurs in Pro-Am competition and observed their play. Most could have improved their ability to swing simply by improving their level of fitness. Lack of flexibility and strength limits so many players from reaching their golf potential, especially seniors and ladies.

That is why I'm happy to see my friend, Gary Wiren, offer this book on adding length to your game. Because he recognizes as I do the importance of the condition of the human body in producing consistently good golf shots, I couldn't agree more with Gary that "training for golf" is one of the next movements in golf that the serious player will incorporate to improve his or her game. I most heartily endorse that concept and encourage you to participate. You'll see the difference in your performance.

Gary Player

Gary Player

INTRODUCTION

If you want to hit a golf ball farther than you do now regardless of your age, handicap level, or physical condition, this book can help you do it. That's not just a lightly considered promise. It's a statement based upon my study of the power golf swing for many years and my experience in applying that knowledge to my own swing and the swings of thousands of other golfers.

I am Gary Wiren, 48 years of age, the National Director of Learning and Research for the Professional Golfers' Association of America. I am a golf professional and have taught golf to more than 500,000 people. I have a Doctorate in Physical Education. My doctoral dissertation was written on "Human Factors Influencing the Golf Drive for Distance." So you can readily understand my interest and why, for more than twenty years, I have been concentrating on the solution to the problem of driving a golf ball farther.

At 5 feet 11 inches and 185 pounds, I am not a "gorilla." But you will discover in reading this book, I am reasonably strong as a result of an exercise program that I have conscientiously carried out for many years.

Recently in the 1983 National Long Drive Competition I won the local qualifying round with a hit of 381 yards 1 foot. The wind was behind me on that drive, but even allowing for its help that shot was 50 yards beyond my nearest competitor. It was most satisfying to realize that at this stage in my life I could accomplish such a feat. I am still learning new things about my swing, working on it, and improving it. That is the underlying theme of this book. If I can do it, you can do it, too, if you want to badly enough. We are going to try to show you how.

I have always been fascinated by physical feats that require great strength. It has amazed me that people could drive spikes into boards with their bare hands, lift heavy weights from the floor, bend bars of metal, or pull a row of railroad cars along a track. The act of hitting a golf ball a prodigious distance appears to be just as awe-inspiring to a multitude of golfers. After all, driving a golf ball 300 to 350 yards is a physical accomplishment that should not go unrecognized. It requires a golf club head to be traveling some 135 mph and produces thousands of pounds of force at impact.

Performers of great feats of strength generally stand out from the crowd physically. They are usually extremely muscularly endowed or, if they lack muscle definition, have massive bulk that disguises their power. This is not necessarily true in the case of golfers. Some of the longest hitters in the world have not been large people. Before his automobile accident in 1952, Ben Hogan, at 5'7", 145 pounds, was the winner of many long drive contests. So was Juan "Chi Chi" Rodriguez at 5'6", and 138 pounds. Anyone can understand how George Bayer at 6'5", 255 pounds, would be a long hitter, but how does one explain how the smaller people can perform equally well?

When I started looking more closely at the matter back in the mid 1960s, it seemed as though the golf literature offered a variety of explanations. When they were interviewed on the subject of distance, great players made conflicting remarks. Tommy Armour talked about hands as his source of power; Bobby Jones his timing; Jack Nicklaus his legs; and Bobby Nichols his back muscles. The fact is that there is no one set of muscles or a single movement that is responsible. It is a combination of factors that work to create distance—with each individual emphasizing his or her own particular strengths.

At the age of thirteen I attended my first golf clinic at a dirt tee public course where an honest-to-goodness PGA professional (the first one I'd ever seen) was giving the lesson. The teacher was a proper Englishman who still played in knickers and possessed one of those classic "turn in a barrel" swings that produced a beautiful repeating draw. Unfortunately his drive traveled only about 215 yards after a full roll. When he finished his demonstration he asked some of us "kids" in the gallery to give it a try. I accepted the challenge and stepped up to the tee. With my ugly caddy grip, closed stance, and overswing, I caught a beauty that drove the ball about 20 yards past his. "That's not the way you do it," was the next line I heard—and was summarily dismissed in favor of a shorter hitter.

I smile now as I recall that incident because the attitude toward instructing young players today is more to: "Teach them to hit it a long way; and when they've learned that, we'll teach them to hit it straight."

There is no question that heredity plays a large part in your present ability or potential ability to drive the golf ball for distance. Who could argue otherwise? But how about getting the most out of what you have? The development of sound technique and the maintenance and strengthening of your body are two of the critical factors that will influence your ability to reach your potential. That's all any of us can hope to do.

Let me give you a couple of examples of different approaches that accomplished the same result. In 1964 Michael Warren Davis, 5'10" tall and weighing 160 pounds, came to the University of Oregon as a freshman. We put him on a training program that included a specially constructed progressively weighted driver. Within two years he won the NCAA Long Drive Contest.

More recently one of my pupils, Sue Pierce Biago, a reasonably long driver after improving her technique, added an additional 20 yards to her drive through an intensive course on Nautilus weight training equipment. The interesting part of Sue's story is that when she interrupts her training regime for any period of time, her club control and distance both diminish noticeably.

You will be given a complete training program in this book. You may not wish to do all the exercises; you may not have the time to do them. But even if you select a part of the program that you can fit into your life—just 10 minutes, three times a week— I promise you that you will see a noticeable difference in the length of your drives in the future.

Golf's "golden steps" are those you take when you walk past your opponent's drive. You'll be taking them more often if you read and practice the material in this book.

Gary Wiren

Gary Wiren

CO-AUTHOR'S STATEMENT

I believe that I am indirectly the "father" of this book. For more than 20 years I have been writing on the history of golf and on the techniques of golf and bowling. You may be aware of some of my books on the Masters, on St. Andrews, and the instructional book *Inside Golf* among others, but that does not really matter.

I have been a low handicap player all my adult life. I had excellent instruction when I was young and captained the University of Detroit golf team in 1935 and 1936. I hold two nine-hole amateur course records—one at the Detroit Golf Club and one at Atlantis in Florida.

I am 5 feet 7 inches tall and weigh 168 pounds. All my life I have fought the battle of the long ball. Achieving anything more than adequate distance always escaped me. Having sold my auto agency and retired from Detroit to Florida in 1969, I thought I'd have time to lick the problem, but found myself playing golf in a most unsatisfactory manner.

I was giving in to age (52 at that time), taking a 3-iron where I once took a 5-iron and using the "old man's friend," the 7-

wood. My handicap had risen to 7, and I saw nothing but further deterioration in view.

Then I happened to play golf one day at Atlantis with Gary Wiren. On the second hole of the east nine I saw him carry a lake at the 275-yard mark. At the seventh hole I saw him carry over trees at a dogleg and put his ball into a greenside bunker on a hole that measures 356 yards. I found this hard to believe, but it was true. This young man was hitting the ball farther than I had ever seen done before.

At lunch that day Gary told me about his study of long driving. I was most interested in view of my own problem of losing distance. Subsequently Gary let me read his doctoral thesis and also described some of the exercises he suggested I use to increase my distance.

He explained how important it was that through exercise I increase the arc of my swing, get a better turn, and be able to retain the hit until later in my swing. I took his advice about the exercises, and since then I have faithfully carried out a regime of stretching and using a heavy golf club.

The results of this long campaign to increase my driving distance have been most satisfying. I'll never drive the ball prodigious distances I know; but on the other hand, there isn't a long 4-par I can't reach in two strokes these days, some of them with iron seconds. I am averaging 225 to 230 yards on my drives with an occasional perfect one to the 250 mark. These are measured drives, I want to assure you, usually measured by my opponents who find it hard to believe that I have increased my driving distance so dramatically. My present 3 handicap at age 66 is much more enjoyable, and the 69 I shot two weeks ago was pure delight.

This leads to the statement about my "fathering" this book. I realized what Gary Wiren had done for my driving ability and told him many times he should write this book so he could help other golfers the way he helped me.

At last he agreed to write it provided I helped him find the time to put it together. Most gladly I agreed. The book in your hands today is the pleasant result.

One final statement: This is Gary Wiren's book on how to drive the golf ball a long, long way. The "I" speaking represents the thoughts and voice of Gary Wiren.

I sincerely hope the book will add as much to your enjoyment of golf as the ideas in it have added to mine.

Dawson Taylor

Bobby Jones

"There are more than a few golfers in this land who wonder why, and how it is, that even when they connect sweetly with a drive, it never goes as far as an ordinary shot by a youth of much less physical power."

1
THERE IS NO *ONE* PERFECT GOLF SWING

Man has always been fascinated by the challenge of the unknown, the resolutions of apparently insoluble problems, some worthy, some capricious. One persistent enigma that has tantalized the minds and tested the skills of golfers since the seventeenth century has been the search for *the perfect golf swing*—particularly one that combines accuracy with power.

Hundreds, possibly thousands, of devotees of the game have invested their time and talent toward this rewarding goal but no one man has dedicated his enthusiasm and financial resources in such a grand manner as did the English gentleman Sir Ainsley Bridgland. Wealthy in his own right, a "keen" golfer, and of questioning mind, Sir Ainsley had a haunting feeling that there must be some hidden secret in the game of golf, some simple key that would unlock for him and possibly for all golfers the treasure house of the perfect swing. Certainly, he reasoned, if the swing was carefully studied under controlled conditions with the latest in engineering aids like high-speed photography, the secret would be revealed. That is precisely what he set out to do.

With the cooperation of the Golf Society of Great Britain, Bridgland sponsored the formation of a first-rate team of specialists representing many different disciplines: biomechanics, engineering, anatomy, physiology, ballistics, medicine, physical education, and ergonomics (the application of engineering data to problems relating to the adjustment of man and the machine). Needless to say, Bridgland believed that with a team such as he had assembled, the answer to his quest would inevitably be found.

The team of experts experimented, discussed, and analyzed the various elements of the game of golf for more than five years. The results of their work culminated in the publication in 1968 of the most fascinating technical book ever written on the golf swing. The authors were physicist/author Alistair Cochran and golf writer John Stobbs. The book was called *The Search for the Perfect Swing.*

Unfortunately for Bridgland and for all golfers, the search for a particular "secret" of the golf swing was not successful. The reams of experimental test data, mathematical models, hypotheses, computer printouts, and high-speed camera work did not provide Bridgland with the answer he wanted. The conclusion of all the studies, on the other hand, was this: Although a model can be constructed that exemplifies sound principles in the golf swing, *there is no perfect golf swing* for all. The idea of there being one perfect swing for distance or direction is a myth. Instead, the conclusion was that there are many variables that are functional and can be considered correct as long as they do not violate physical law. That is why you see a variety of swing styles among the greatest players in the world. It is also one of the reasons why there is a variety of opinion about why some people can produce prodigious drives and others can't.

There must be individualism in swinging a golf club. However, such individualism can never give license to employ a technique that violates physical law or basic principle. For example, it would be wrong to teach golfers to use a grip with both hands facing the sky, because such a grip would restrict angular motion and leverage in the swing. That grip might be very effective for putting or even chipping where maximum clubhead velocity is not a factor. But it would violate a physical principle if it were applied to the full golf swing.

Even a casual study of the game's greatest performers should convince the most stubborn advocate of a single swing style that individual differences do exist. The only *absolute* statement you can make about the swings of great golfers is that they all are different. Some are similar looking, I'll agree. All of those good swings share a common ground in principle. But no two swings are exactly the same.

I believe that recognizing the individual differences in students raises teaching to an art. So let's discuss a teaching model that recognizes those differences, one in which method does not overpower or replace result.

This proposed model offers three levels of priority in understanding the golf swing and helps to explain the causative factors in producing distance. Those levels of priority are:

1. Laws
2. Principles
3. Preferences

Each is defined in the following manner:

Law—A statement of an order or relation of phenomena that, so far as is known, is invariable under given conditions. It refers to the physical forces of nature that directly influence the flight of the ball.

Principle—A first cause, or force. It is a factor of high order which must be dealt with and which, in this model, has direct relation to and influence on *law*. Some call it fundamental.

Preference—The act of choosing and liking better some particular approach, method, device, etc., over all others. To be valid in this model, it must relate to *principle*.

THE BALL FLIGHT LAWS

The Ball Flight Laws, assessed at the moment of impact, are these:

1. Speed—The velocity with which the clubhead is traveling influences the distance the ball will be propelled.
2. Centeredness—The point on the clubface where the ball is struck will influence distance and direction.
3. Path—The direction in which the clubhead is moving will influence the direction in which the ball will travel.
4. Face—The degree at which the surface of the clubface, running on a horizontal axis, is at right angles to the swing line will influence the accuracy of the ball's flight.
5. Angle of Attack—The steepness of descent or ascent of the forward swing of the clubhead will influence the trajectory and the distance the ball will travel.

Ball Flight Laws are the most important because they work every time, without fail. The ball is not concerned with the technicalities of swing style. It responds to being struck without any prejudice toward the striker. It doesn't ask what particular swing method is being used nor does it care about handicap, club affiliation, sex, or age. It follows the basic Ball Flight Laws, whether the golfer uses an open or square stance, has a fast or slow backswing, an overlapping or ten-fingered grip, a firm or cupped wrist, or uses leverage or centrifugal force as his or her primary source of power.

Obviously, there are equipment factors such as clubface loft, construction of the ball, material of the hitting surface, that will influence the distance and direction of the ball's flight. Environmental conditions such as temperature, humidity, wind, terrain, and altitude are also recognized as having an effect. In this book, however, we consider only the physical human factors over which we have some control.

PRINCIPLES OF THE SWING

All the aforementioned elements have an important influence on the flight of the ball. That brings us to our second order of priority: Principles.

There are fundamental considerations in the swing that have

a direct bearing on a player's application of the Laws and therefore all influence distance to some degree. They are called *Principles of the Swing*. Whereas the Laws are irrefutable and absolute (at least as absolute as we can be in this relative universe), the Principles reflect subjective judgment on the mechanics of the swing.

Listing these elements does not mean the list is all-inclusive. The Principles are divided into two categories: Pre-Swing and In-Swing.

PRE-SWING PRINCIPLES

1. GRIP

Grip has a significant influence on several of the principles listed. Rotation of the hands less than ½ inch clockwise in the grip can cause the clubface to open enough for a 40-yard slice. A 40-yard off-line shot can cause the player to attempt adjustments in other parts of the swing.

2. AIM

One of the principles that is violated most frequently and often unknowingly by the golfer, *aim* includes both aim of the clubface and aim of the body. Proper body aim or alignment has a strong influence on proper path, though it does not guarantee it.

3. SETUP (Includes posture, ball position, stance, and weight distribution)

Setup influences all five of the ball flight laws: clubhead speed, clubhead path, position of clubface, angle of attack, and sequences of contact. Ball position, for example, affects the angle of attack and trajectory of the shot. A ball played forward in the stance increases the angle of attack and results in a higher shot. A ball played back in the stance has the opposite result. There are similar examples for each segment of setup.

IN-SWING PRINCIPLES

1. DOWNSWING PLANE

The downswing plane is measured by the position of the clubshaft. It is said to be *in plane* and therefore correct when, midway through the downswing, an extension of the butt end of the club would intersect a line drawn through the ball to the target line. If the butt end of the club points outside the intended flight line, the clubhead will travel from inside to outside. If it points inside, the swing will be from outside to inside.

2. LEFT WRIST POSITION (The relationship between the back of the left hand and the back of the left forearm)

By cupping or arching the left wrist, the clubface position can be dramatically influenced. Mechanically, the simplest method is to allow the wrist to cock but in a plane that keeps the left hand and wrist in a flat plane throughout the swing. This, however, is physically difficult to accomplish by many golfers.

3. WIDTH OF ARC

If the golfer allows his left arm to bend before impact, his clubhead speed is reduced because the lever length is shortened. It is the same principle that causes the middle portion of a spoke on a wheel to travel more slowly than the far end of the spoke even though the force emanating from the axle is the same.

4. LENGTH OF ARC

Limiting the length of the backswing basically limits the distance the golf ball can be driven. For example, consider the length of the backswing for a short putt and contrast it to that of a 20-yard pitch shot. The longer backswing obviously produces more potential for distance. There is such a thing as taking the club back too far and losing control, but the reverse, too short a backswing, is by far the more common problem.

5. LEVER SYSTEM*

A swing without cocking the wrist is a one-lever system. By adding a second lever to the wrist cock, the golfer approximately doubles his potential force.

6. TIMING (Things happening in the swing in the order they should)

The backswing should overlap in this order: (1) hands, (2) arms, (3) shoulders, (4) hips, (5) legs—then the forearm swing should return 5, 4, 3, 2, 1, in sequence and in rhythm. When this sequence in rhythm occurs, the greatest possible force is unleashed.

7. RELEASE

The momentum of the club causes the arms and hands to make a natural release when the ball is struck. Proper release can be inhibited if there is undue muscular tension. Conscious attempts to hit hard cause hand and forearm tension. The resulting muscle tightness stops a natural release and keeps the clubface open.

8. DYNAMIC BALANCE (The ability to transfer the body weight from the right to the left in your through swing while maintaining body control)

Nearly all good players use the footwork common to all striking and throwing actions, the movement from the back to the front foot in delivering the blow. Remaining on the back foot reduces the power of the swing and changes the path and arc of the swing. Failure to get the weight over the rear leg on the backswing reduces the player's power.

---

*(Actually there are several systems of levers operating in the golf swing. The primary one is that formed by the left arm and the club. When the wrist cocks in place with the forearm, the result is a two-lever system.)

9. SWING CENTER
(That point in the body around which the arc of the swing is made. It is located between the shoulders under the top of the sternum or breastbone.)

Technically the golf swing is an ellipse, but it is close to being a circle. When the center is moved the arc of the circle moves, and striking the ball consistently is extremely difficult.

PREFERENCES

The final level of fundamentals is the most practical because it is the level at which we most often work. It is labeled *Preferences.* Those would include, under the Principle of Set-Up, the choices of open, closed, or square stance; wide or narrow foot position; and weight on heels or toward toes. There are literally thousands of combinations.

EXAMPLE A

Let's put all three levels together.
Law: Speed
Principle: Two-Lever System. When you transfer from a one-lever system (which would occur if you tried to swing the golf club with no wrist cock) to a two-lever system created by the left arm and club as the wrist is cocked, you multiply the potential force by approximately 2.3.
Preference: If you need more than one lever in the arm and club relationship, the question is where should you create this second lever, or where should you cock your wrist? Early? In midswing? At the top of the swing? On the downswing? Or even before you start the backswing? That's a *preference.*

The body is behind the ball in the backswing, weight over the right leg, ready to strike forward.

EXAMPLE B

Law: Squareness

Principle: Grip

Preference: Should the pupil use a three-knuckle grip? Two-knuckle? Overlapping? Interlocking? Full-fingered? Cross-handed? Strong pressure? Light pressure? Again the answer will depend on the individual. Some experimentation might be necessary to find the right combination of grip elements that will produce the desired ball flight.

When you consider the Preference category the possibilities are limitless. Examine the preferences you find in many excellent golf swings. Consider the following: Should the shoulders be aimed to the left, the center, or the right of the target? Should the stance be open, square, or closed? Should the weight be back or forward at address? Should the left or right side be favored? Is the ball position variable or standard? Should the address be relaxed or taut? Is it a flat, medium, or upright plane? Is the left arm bent or straight at the top of the backswing? Is the backswing short or long? Is the left wrist cupped, flat, or arched?

Is the face open, square, or shut to the tangent of the arc? Is the swing-through initiated with the feet, knees, legs, hips, arms, or hands? Is the hip movement lateral, circular, or both? Do the forearms rotate to provide release or is it the wrists, or both? Where is the weight distributed during the swing? Does the left knee straighten on the downswing or stay flexed? Does the head move laterally, up, or down?

Where the Laws are fixed in number, the Principles are limited, but the Preferences reach a staggering total. The point is, there are a great many techniques and combinations of techniques that can work and do work. One objective of this book is to help you find the right ones that will give you the most functional power.

Julius Boros

"How do I hit the ball so far when I swing so easy? The answer is simple. I hit hard. Notice I didn't say I swing hard. The distance your ball travels is governed solely by the amount of power you unleash at impact."

2
THE FOUNDATIONS OF A POWER GOLF SWING

THE WHOLE PICTURE

I like to think of the golf swing as a jigsaw puzzle in motion. We all know that no jigsaw puzzle is complete until the last piece is inserted into the overall picture. We also know that if any one piece of the puzzle is missing, the picture will never be completed satisfactorily.

The principle of the jigsaw puzzle applies as well to the golf swing. It is put together with many separate pieces or elements and yet when all of the parts come together properly the result is a smooth, rhythmic, effective, and powerful golf swing.

In the following chapters we will focus on the individual parts of the golf swing, but you must not conclude that the swing is a disjointed mixture of many separate pieces or movements. It is not. An automobile engine is made of many working parts, but when they are all put together properly the result is a single entity, a well-functioning machine that delivers power smoothly to the driving wheels of a car.

We can examine closely a particular part of a car engine, such as the function of a piston, without losing sight of the fact that it is merely an important, vital part of the complete engine. In the same way, we propose to examine the parts of the golf swing. When they are understood and assembled intelligently they result in the completed jigsaw puzzle, a golf swing that is efficient, repeating, and powerful enough to drive a golf ball a great distance.

THE PROPER GRIP

There has been a great deal of discussion and even controversy for many years over the proper way to grip a golf club. You have heard golfers talk of the overlapping or Vardon grip, the baseball grip, the interlocking grip, and about strong and weak positions of the hands. It is most important that you understand the basic elements of each one of these grips so you can make your own decision about the way you should grip the golf club most effectively and swing it with the greatest efficiency and power.

Early photographs of the golfers of the 1800s tell us that they held the golf club with both hands positioned similarly to the way an ordinary person would grip an axe, that is, with the handle in the palms with no locking or overlapping of the fingers but the hands held as close together as possible. It was obvious even in the early days of golf that the closer the hands the more the "hit" at the golf ball was a unified effort, that is, one in which neither hand was more in control of the swing than the other at the moment of striking.

Then, in the 1890s, a great golf champion, John Henry Taylor (a Scotsman who was always called "J.H."), discovered that if he overlapped the little finger of his right hand with the forefinger of his left hand, he could achieve consistently more compactness in his grip. Another great golfer of that day, Harry Vardon, adopted Taylor's new grip idea, and when Vardon won tournament after tournament using it, the public began to call the grip the "Vardon grip." To this day, it is probably the grip most universally used by golfers.

There are notable exceptions, of course. The most prominent nonuser of the Vardon grip today is the great modern champion Jack Nicklaus, who does not have large hands. He uses a finger interlocking grip with tremendous success. Senior players Bob Rosburg, former PGA Champion and Art Wall, former Masters Champion, use the ten-fingered or baseball grip. And there are other excellent golfers who, for one reason or another, have found they need to grip the club in what might be considered an unorthodox fashion in order to swing the club most effectively.

Henry Picard, Masters Champion of 1937 and PGA Champion of 1938, injured his left thumb just before he played in the Masters of 1937. He decided to move his left thumb outside of his grip to lessen the pressure on it. The grip worked so well that Henry won that Masters and ever afterward used the same grip. That same grip has been Gene Sarazen's for a lifetime.

Players who have short fingers sometimes feel that the amount of overlap afforded them in the Vardon grip is not sufficient to unitize the hands and they prefer an interlocking style like Nicklaus to achieve that meld. This is a very compact grip, and after the overlapping "Vardon" grip, it may be the next most common grip in general use among golfers of the world.

The ten-fingered or modified baseball grip is just what the name implies, a grip with all the fingers plus the two thumbs used on the grip. There is no interconnection between the hands as in the Vardon grip with its little finger of the right making a connection by overlapping the forefinger of the left. Those who have very small hands, or who seek more leverage rather than centrifugal force, find that the baseball grip offering greater speed is more satisfactory than any other for them.

Here is an experiment I would like you to try. It will illustrate the necessity for the two hands to work together as a unit in the golf swing. Take a club in your hands and grip it with a 2-inch separation between the top hand (your left, if you play right-handed) and your right or bottom hand. Try to swing at an imaginary ball with that grip. Notice how the right hand suddenly overpowers the left as it nears the bottom of the swing. Now, for a second experiment, slide your two hands as close together on

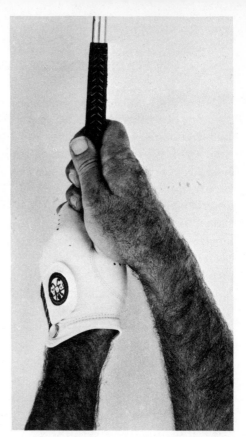

The most common "neutral" grip. The "V" of the right hand points between the chin and right shoulder. The left hand shows two knuckles.

the shaft as you are able. Try another swing. You will see that the hands are getting closer to working as a unit rather than separately.

What we are seeking in the effective golf grip is a pair of hands opposed to each other on the golf shaft but opposed to each other in such a way that neither hand overpowers the other. You want your two hands to work together as a unit. You want a compact grip, not one in which one or the other of your hands is working separately. Usually one side of a person's body is more developed and thus stronger than the other. The right-handed person usually has a stronger right hand than left. The reverse is true for the natural left-hander. Because the right hand delivers quite a strong blow at the ball, it is necessary for the left hand, left wrist, and left side of the body to be strong enough not to let the right hand take control and overpower the left before or at the moment of impact. In this book you will find my suggestions for exercises that will attempt to balance the right and left side power.

It is most important that you find the grip style that gives you *unity of hands,* one where there is no separation during the swing, no letting go, and where there is a balance of power. When you have settled on the right grip for you, you are well on your way to building a powerful golf swing.

Let's discuss the position of the fingers in a good golf grip. Some of the fingers are of greater importance in the grip than others. These are the last three fingers of the left hand and the third and fourth fingers of the right hand. There is also an important *trigger point* in the pad of the right forefinger.

The club must be held in the left hand so that it lies across the fingers at the bottom on the left hand (the first and second fingers) and then rides upward across the hand, eventually to be held firmly against the pad of the left hand. It is of the utmost importance that the golfer build as much strength as possible in the last three fingers of his left hand. The left hand and those last three fingers are the primary controllers of the clubface position, thus influencing the degree of accuracy you have to accompany your length. The hands and fingers must be strong enough to withstand the considerable impact of the clubhead as it strikes the ball. Since the ball is often struck at a point off-center from the clubface, a strong twisting effect results, a torque

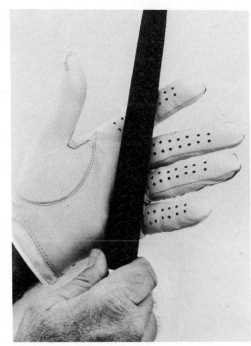

The club's grip runs across the base of the last two fingers of the left hand where you can most effectively trap it against the fleshy pad of that hand.

which attempts to force the clubhead to turn clockwise. In addition, it has been demonstrated with individuals on electronic speed timers that those with more strength and mass to resist the rebound effect of the club at impact drive farther than those with equal clubhead speed but less resistance. With a strong left hand and fingers, the golfer can reduce the torque and rebound and keep the clubhead on line through impact and follow-through. So in Chapter 5, you'll see specific attention paid to forearm and finger development.

Where the little finger of the right hand may be used to unify the grip by overlapping or interlocking, the other three fingers of the right hand are of great importance, too. The club shaft lies more in the fingers of the right hand than it does in the left. Here is why.

Gripping the club into the palm of the right hand tends to freeze the wrist from hinging at the top of the swing. It is this hinging action that provides you with additional potential power for clubhead speed. It's easy to visualize this. Extend your right hand out in front of you as though you were shaking hands. Now swing your arm back as though you were going to slap someone or something, but tighten your forearm so your right wrist won't hinge. Imagine the slap . . . or better, have someone extend his hand from the other direction and you actually slap it. Now try again, but this time relax the muscles in your forearm and let your wrist hinge as your arm swings back. Repeat the slap. As you'll see, it will be with greater force.

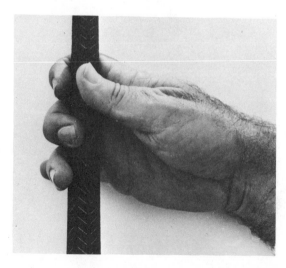

The right hand employs a finger grip for the best release.

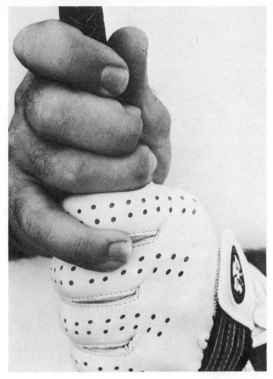

The standard overlapping grip

When you grip the club more in the fingers of the right hand it will allow you to get this setting/cocking movement in your hand and wrist.

Like so many things in golf the feeling you get from this kind of grip is the opposite of what you'd expect. It feels weak but is actually strong because it will produce more consistent clubhead speed.

Placing the grip in the fingers of the right hand causes the club to lie between the first and second joints of the index finger. The fleshy pad just above the second joint is an important pressure point applied against the shaft and is another reason why the right hand finger grip is crucial.

In the Vardon grip the little finger of the right hand overlaps the left index finger, either riding on top of it or else by sliding down into the slot between the first and second fingers of the left hand. (See photos.) Today some form of the overlapping grip is used by 90 to 95 percent of the low-handicap golfers of the world.

I suggest that you experiment with each grip to see if there is a difference. In my case, I grip the club with my little finger

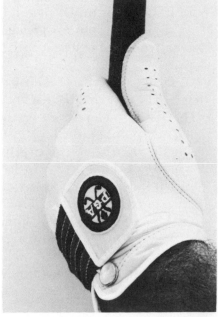

A variation of the overlap grip is the interlock (right). Below left: A long-thumb grip in the left hand tightens the forearm flexors. The swing becomes less wristy, more of an arm swing. Below right: The short thumb in the left hand puts the club shaft at more of a diagonal and increases the use of hands and wrists.

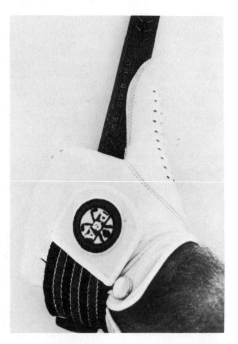

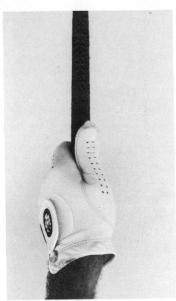

Above, left: This is a neutral or natural left-hand grip, which is a good one for most people. Two knuckles of the back of the left hand are visible. At right is a natural left-thumb position where the club runs at a slight diagonal across the hand. This thumb position is a little longer than a true short-thumb position.

Below at left is left-handed grip showing three knuckles. This grip encourages a closed clubface. At center is a grip that encourages a closed face or "hook." The "V" of the right hand points to the right shoulder; the left hand shows three knuckles. At right is a grip that discourages hooking. The "V" of the right hand is pointing to the chin, and only one knuckle of the left hand is visible.

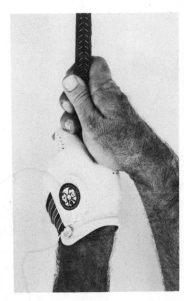

sliding down into the slot between the forefinger and the third finger of my left hand. Ben Hogan gripped his club that way, Tom Watson does, and so do thousands of other golfers whose names you'd recognize.

PROPER AIM AND SETUP

What are we trying to do when we make a golf swing? The answer, of course, is that we are trying to drive a golf ball from *here,* a spot on the ground in front of us, to *there,* to a definite target—the center of the fairway on a long hole, the green on a long 3 par hole, the flagstick and the hole itself as we near the green.

On every shot in golf, the golfer is aiming or should be aiming at a target. The golfer must have a target in mind, a spot on the fairway or green where he can see "in his mind's eye" where his ball will land.

Accurate hitting of the target in golf requires a swing that consistently delivers the clubface square to the line toward the target. The best way to achieve that "squareness to the line" is to swing the club from inside the target line. The golfer may have the *feeling* that he is hitting from inside the line to the outside.

In a correct inside swing you should imagine that you are part of a large wheel that rotates first to the right in your backswing and then to the left in your downswing. The club moves around your body like a spoke of that wheel with the clubhead traveling on the outer rim of the wheel. In order to achieve this wheel-like body motion, the arms remain close to the right side of the body. It is obvious, too, that the center of that wheel, believed to be a point somewhere near the top of the spine, does not move to the right or left, up or down. In other words, the axis of that swing must remain steady, in a turning motion which allows the body, arms, and hands to make a swing that will return the clubface to precisely the place from which it started in the backswing.

The way you address the ball is most important because it involves physical comfort, correct aiming, and relaxation of

Alignment of the left shoulder is a primary factor in influencing the path. Above left, Dawson uses a club to help Detroit Golf Club Ladies' champ Mary Last. Notice that the shoulder is exaggerated in its aim to the right, encouraging the swing to follow an inside path out to the right of the target. Above right, an open-shoulder position with the left shoulder aiming to the left of target will encourage the swing path to follow that line to the left of target. At left: A square position in which the shoulder, hip, and foot line parallel the intended flight line will encourage the swing path to travel toward the target.

tension. Each golfer should observe the same aiming routine every time he makes a shot. He should walk up from behind the ball on the line to the target. He should study the target and target line for a moment. Then with that line clearly in mind he should step into his address position.

Stand to the ball so that it is directly between your feet, and then widen your feet about the width of your shoulders. Take your grip, first with your left hand and then with your right, and allow your arms to hang straight down so that, from the front, you are in a perfectly "square-to-the-line" position as far as your head, shoulders, arms, legs, and feet are concerned.

Standing too close to the ball inhibits power by restricting the release.

In an attempt to get more power, a golfer will often stand too far away from the ball. The result is frequently a loss of power, as the tendency is to hit the ball with the arms independent of the body.

Trying to keep the head still over the ball frequently results in a reverse weight shift at the top of the swing and a substantial loss of power.

Now, bend over the ball. Put yourself in a slight "sitting-down" attitude. Your knees should be slightly bent and relaxed. Your tailbone should stick out a bit. The head is not dropped but should be brought up slightly so as to allow continued observation of the target line.

Every golfer has to find his own proper address position. We all vary in our physical makeup. Some of us have longer arms than others, some people are long-waisted and short-legged. Others are just the reverse, short-waisted and long-legged. Each one of these physical attributes will affect the final combination of hands, arms, legs, and body in the golf swing.

In the beginning, you should position the ball on a line that runs at a true right angle to the target line in a range directly out from the inside of your left heel to a position 2 or 3 inches more centered. Probably 80 percent of all golfers use this line and ball position with success. The reason is that it allows the clubhead to reach maximum acceleration just before it strikes the ball.

Furthermore, most golfers seem to feel most comfortable with the ball placed there.

However, remember that another 10 percent of all golfers find their best success with the ball positioned either forward of that inner left shoe line or behind it. Less flexible people may have it placed farther back, while those more flexible may have it a bit more forward. Don't be locked into a set ball position. Try various positions until you come to your own conclusion on the spot that allows you to hit the ball harder, straighter, and more consistently.

Be aware that as you place the ball forward in your stance, (more off the toe of your left foot) you increase the difficulty of keeping your left wrist from breaking down as you hit the ball. It will become more difficult for you to keep the clubhead square to the target line and to keep the clubhead moving down that line as it strikes the ball.

The reverse may be true as you experiment with moving the ball backward in your stance, more toward the center of your body. You will find that it will become more and more difficult for you to get your clubface back to square with the ball as it strikes it. With your clubface not closed, your shots may start going to the right. Or, you may unconsciously attempt to force the clubface back to square and end up smothering the shot or hooking the ball badly to the left.

I suggest that you experiment to find your best ball position at address. Try the conventional spot first, near your inner left heel, and work out your swing from there. If that does not work satisfactorily for you, try moving the ball forward first, before you try the positions farther back to the right. My best advice to you and to all golfers is that you trust your professional teacher to analyze your swing and help you find not only the best position of the ball at address but also every other "best position" for you in grip, in stance, at the top of your backswing, and in the other fundamentals of the swing.

THE UNHURRIED BACKSWING

It is helpful to start your backswing leisurely. In my teaching career I have seen only a few pupils who actually swung back too slowly. If a mistake was made it was quite likely that the backswing was much too fast. Too much speed in the backswing seldom allows you to get to a solid position from which to return your swing. Frequently, fast backswings will be too short. The rush in the backswing is made in an attempt to get speed in the hitting area. When the backswing length is too short to build momentum on the forward swing, then there is a flurry of activity, hurrying back in order to get through to the finish.

When Jack Nicklaus needed to drive the 4-par eighteenth hole at St. Andrews in the British Open of 1970, he said that he kept telling himself before he made the shot, "swing slowly, swing slowly." We know that he did drive the green and that shot helped him to win over Doug Sanders.

The clubhead starts back best on a line roughly parallel to the golfer's shoulder alignment. If the club is snatched away in a quick, hurried movement, the relationship is destroyed at once and usually cannot be recaptured by any other compensating move.

When a golfer swings back too quickly, snatches the club away from the ball, he chokes off his arm swing and body turn. It is most important that you be in control of the club, not it in control of you. It's a back swing, not a back lift, back push, or back jerk. Those things happen when the club is taken away in too rapid a backswing. When the club is jerked away at the beginning of the swing, it almost inevitably follows that it will be rushed on the downswing as well.

It *is* possible to start your backswing *too slowly*. Too slow a tempo causes you to rush the forward swing in an attempt to pick up speed. But I would rather see you swinging back leisurely, almost deliberately, for a while until you have impressed upon your mind the necessity of a swinging motion away from the ball, attempting to get a full windup and stretch. Then find the proper tempo that fits your swing and personality.

At the same time that I am urging you to swing back in an unhurried manner, I recommend that you start forward the same way. When I am driving my best, I have the feeling of getting set in a good position at the top of my swing and then

Here is a square-face position at the top. Note the flat wrist. The natural return from this position encourages a straight shot and the confidence to hit a powerful one.

Here is an open-face position at the top. Note the cupped wrist, which encourages a slice.

Compare the shut-face position on the left to the open face on the right. Neither is preferred.

This is a closed-face position at the top. Note the arched wrist, which encourages a hook.

starting down as casually as I can. The acceleration starts to build up at once, of course, but the start down is not hurried.

RHYTHM AND BALANCE

The word "rhythm" comes to us from ancient Greek and originally meant "music." It denotes a regularly patterned flow in physical activities. Maybe that's why some of our early great golf teachers used music in their lessons. The late Ernest Jones always used music and produced good player after good player. In our PGA Discovery Schools we use it for that very reason, rhythm and free-flowing movement. When we say that the golf swing must have rhythm or be rhythmical, we mean that each separate golf swing should have the same regular pattern flow

If the width of the arc is lost at the top of the swing (here seen caused by a severely bent left elbow), it is difficult to recapture coming down. Some bend in the left arm may be necessary, however, in the case of the stocky or less flexible individual.

The hips and pelvis should turn so the weight is over the right leg, which is the primary pivot point in the backswing.

from the moment the golfer steps into his stance and the golf swing begins until the golf ball is sent on its way and the swing comes to its natural conclusion. This is the critical link action chain of events that produces power. The term "rhythmical" applies to the consistent repetition of the same coordinated, measured golf swing time after time in an identical pattern, swing after swing.

This rhythmical swing is best seen in the swings of the great golfers of our time. One of the finest examples of a repeating rhythmical golf swing is that of Sam Snead, winner of more PGA events than anyone in history. Whether he is hitting a full drive, a medium iron, or a short pitch shot, Snead always exhibits the same smooth, almost leisurely tempo in his swing. But the results he gets with his smooth swing pay off in a consistently high acceleration of clubhead speed and beautiful golf shots, long and accurate.

The golfer's body in some swing styles moves from left to right and back to the left again in rhythmic sequence as he "feels" his proper balance from the soles of his feet up through his whole body. As this feeling of balance and rhythm pervades the entire body, the initial movement may come for a *forward press,* of hands and right knee to the left, a sort of kickoff that starts the club and the body into a reactive motion in a smooth takeaway from the ball in the other direction.

For most players the forward press or kickoff of the swing is a completely unconscious maneuver, an instinctive one that does not require any particular attention of the mind.

The next time you watch the stars of golf in action, pay particular attention to the various individual ways they perform the forward press. Gary Player's is particularly noticeable as he *kicks* his right knee in toward the ball. Jack Nicklaus's forward press is less obvious, a firming of his grip as he starts the club back and a rotation of his head to the right at the same time.

Not all good players use a forward press nor do they all go in a left, right, left pattern with their weight. Some set up their upper body more to the right, particularly on a tee shot, and then simply wind over the right leg and shift back to the left. The choice of style can be likened to the baseball pitcher. Some throw from a stretch with no one on base, others use a windup. Are they seeking velocity, accuracy, or a blend? That's the same question you have to answer.

Whichever setup you choose (favoring left, balanced, or favoring right), I recommend that you practice swinging to a rhythm count or beat. You can count to yourself as you swing, like—"one, and two!" *One* is your backswing; *and* is your top and change of direction; *two* your forward motion. Music might also help. Small cassette recorders make music very accessible. A waltz might feel comfortable, or perhaps you would like something more contemporary to encourage a good golf rhythm.

You must perfect your rhythm in order to consistently drive the golf ball a long way. It must be the same rhythm swing after swing, for, as we have discussed, any interruption of that rhythm means a likely breakdown in the link action or proper timing and a subsequent loss of clubhead speed.

Your ultimate success at long driving depends upon many different factors: increased flexibility which will give you a wider, longer arc; a sound platform from which to "launch your projectile," the speeding clubhead aided by a strong musculature; and many others. But good rhythm that promotes *balance* and helps produce a proper sequencing of the swing is a strong foundation upon which to build.

Balance comes from a proper setup, sound footwork, and from swinging "within yourself," that is, at a pace your body and temperament can handle. How often we have seen inexperienced players swing much too hard at the ball and fall off balance.

I recommend that you watch the good players as they swing in balance. Pay particular attention to the way the left knee and left foot work inward to the right on the backswing and how the right knee and right foot move forward to the left during the downswing. Try to absorb and imitate the tempo of one of the players whose game you especially admire. The tall player should observe his counterpart on the PGA tour, a player like Nick Faldo, Andy Bean, or Tom Weiskopf. The shorter player should study Tom Watson, Tom Kite, or Larry Nelson.

I would like to call your attention to a teaching device called *Sybervision*. It is a video cassette that features the graceful and balanced swing of past PGA Champion Al Geiberger. His swing was chosen for the teaching series because it is one of the most classic and simple in the golf world today.

On this cassette the same Geiberger swing is shown over and over and over again. Each swing is exactly the same. Al is shown at full length from head on making a full drive, then from behind, down the line, where swing plane becomes so evident. His rhythm and balance are magnificent, helping you also to appreciate the acceleration and release in his swing. By studying Geiberger's swing and watching the tape regularly, the mind becomes kinesthetically brainwashed with his rhythm and technique. It becomes clear in your mind how the swing operates. Confusion is swept away and your confidence builds just like when you watch a golf tournament. Seeing the fine swings makes the striking of a ball seem much easier. This clarification in your mind and confidence that accompanies it will allow you to freewheel—and with that to get your best distance. I strongly recommend the concept of *Sybervision* or similar swing modeling programs.

THE MOMENT OF TRUTH

The reversal of the swing at the top, the start-down toward the ball, is in my opinion the toughest move in golf. If it is done in proper fashion, the other motions in the golf swing flow in beautiful rhythmic sequence. It is the link action system from feet to legs, through the trunk, back, shoulders, arms, and hands, all firing in proper sequence, which provides the maximum mechanical efficiency, clubhead speed, and the rhythmic flowing appearance. Under these circumstances you create a summation of forces that provides you with your greatest clubhead speed. The preferences and styles in golf swings will most certainly change in the years ahead, but the order in which the link system works is enduring. You can't improve on an absolute. When this happens correctly: The clubhead accelerates to its greatest speed just as it reaches the impact area and the right hand and arm speed up to square the face of the clubhead.

It is most important that you understand the trigger point in your swing that starts your clubhead on its way back down to the ball. Your backswing has moved a portion of your weight to the right-hand side of the body. You have wound up the muscles of your arms, shoulders, and trunk to the fullest extent possible over your right leg.

Now—begin to drive and unwind this bundle of energy by firing one link at a time. Start by moving laterally toward the target so that you can get your left heel back on the ground. If you have done it correctly, your left knee will separate farther from your right, which remains almost motionless in this first move in the downswing. Resist any temptation to begin to hit the ball with your right hand and arm. I assure you that your right hand and right arm "hit" will be there as it nears impact if you will obey this rule: *Start your downswing with a left-side move.*

As this lateral-rotary weight shift begins, accompanied by a pull-down and forward with your left arm and left side, you will find that those muscles of your body so carefully coiled in the backswing are suddenly sprung loose, freed, and ready to help accelerate the golf club and clubhead along the return path to

Above left: The first move in the downswing is to get the left heel back on the ground and establish some weight to the left side. Above right: Many long hitters will further cock the wrists at the beginning of the downswing. At right: The hands arrive at the ball leading the clubhead. The head stays back.

Above, at left: Breakdown of the left wrist will result in a major power leak. At right: Hitting from the top means losing your forearm clubshaft angle early in the downswing and, with it, a great deal of power.

and through the ball at the impact area. You'll have that free-wheeling slinging feeling.

I do not like the use of the term "hitting zone" because I believe those terms connote a feeling of a hitting swing rather than the idea of flow that produces a swinging hit. That's when the ball merely *happens* to be in the way of the club. I believe the golfer should imagine that he is swinging his clubhead through a hologram; it's an image. He will find no resistance whatsoever at the bottom of the swing, that the golf ball just happens to be in the way of the clubhead and will be sent on its path almost by the accident of being there.

This happens most effectively when the player projects his swing past the ball down the target line a few feet in front of the ball. It's a martial arts principle. If, for example, you were trying to break a board, you must not focus your attention on the board because that will produce tension just before impact, slowing your arm and hand speed. So the martial arts specialist always focuses on a point beyond the board and simply lets the board get in the way of his blow directed to that spot.

The practice of Jack Nicklaus using a spot on the ground in front of the ball as an intermediary target is effective not only for direction but also for distance. It's obvious that trying to swing toward that spot can help you establish a correct swing path. But have you ever considered that it also can free your hit instinct tension since your focus is past the ball?

Let me suggest two mental pictures you can use to train yourself to perform this left-sided maneuver that begins the downswing. The thought I prefer, because it has worked effectively for me for many years, is that I am pulling my left arm forward so that my right elbow will drop toward my pocket. This "keeps the gun loaded" and stores your hit until the time when you can get the most speed from it. I find that the rest of my body obeys this command with the necessary slide and counterclockwise rotation of my lower body, which in turn brings the clubhead to the ball with considerable acceleration.

The other thought is to look down the range or fairway at your target with the feeling that you are going to unwind and sling the club right over your target, much like a hammer or discus thrower would unwind and let it go.

Experiment with both of these trigger thoughts to see if one works for you. Remember that your mind can hold only one thought at a time. The right elbow to pocket thought and the sensation of slinging are both single, positive thoughts. If you will concentrate on using either one in your game, you may discover that you have been able to block out of your mind any thought of hit or mishit and be able to freewheel.

A very important benefit that flows from the left side pulling theory is that it plays down the premature hit instinct of the right side in the swing. This is most useful because, since most of us are right-handed, we instinctively want to apply our right-sided power to the swing, inevitably too soon or in such a manner that the left hand is unable to withstand the force of the right-hand hit and collapses at impact. The result is a mis-hit golf shot, a dreadful slice, or an awful hook.

Hitting from the top also means the clubhead will more than likely arrive ahead of the hands and the weight will be too far toward the rear foot—both causes of power loss.

Recently all-time great Byron Nelson was describing a clinic he gave several years ago. After hitting a bad hook he commented, "Too much right hand." That shot was followed by a slice and Byron's comment again was, "Too much right hand." One spectator couldn't understand, so Byron explained. "On the first shot I hit with too much right hand too early, letting my left wrist break down, which closed the face and hooked the shot. The very next shot I used too much right hand but this time I used it to squeeze and hold the rotation, leaving the clubface open and producing a slice. But both were too much right hand." That's not to say we don't use the right for power, but that most people need to emphasize the left so that the right does not totally dominate.

The most common fault on the downswing is opening the angle between your left forearm and the shaft too early. The club is thrown out and away instead of being held back inside the flight line by the cocked wrists. It is of utmost importance that you feel the weight of the clubhead speed to the ball. Whipping the clubhead means just what it implies. This outward pull is centrifugal force, which operates most effectively when your

Golf's most critical move, the transfer of weight from right to left while maintaining your "loaded" hand, arm, and club position. Note how my right elbow has dropped toward my pocket.

grip pressure is not too tight and you have maintained your wrist cock well into the forward swing.

Not "staying behind the ball" is a common golf swing mistake. It is equivalent to "coming off the ball." Both actions produce power loss and directional loss. In each case, the center of the swing has moved: In the first example, the center has moved past the ball; in the second example, it has moved away from the ball. Although the true center of the swing arc is at a point just above the sternum or breastbone, the head is a functional reference point. The head remains steady and down as the arms and club swing through. Many golfers are so anxious to see what has happened to their shots that they lift their heads much too quickly and spoil the result. You should keep your head down until it turns as a result of the right shoulder coming through, and bring it up naturally. But be careful; keeping your eye on the ball or keeping your head down longer than after the natural release occurs will destroy sound footwork, good body action, and a complete finish. Don't ever look at the ground at the finish of your follow-through. Look at the target down the fairway.

Some teachers will claim that what you do after you strike the ball has no influence on the result. Technically, they are correct but realistically, the practice of finishing your swing in good balance lends a great assist to what happens at the moment of impact. I recommend it especially for adding distance, because a follow-through that finishes short of a full finish has had to slow down somewhere earlier in the downswing in order to come to a halt prematurely. Likewise, the follow-through that finishes off-balance has been caused by a swing center that has moved too far, a faulty swing plane, or a mistimed application of power. With a good, powerful swing the finish should be natural, uninhibited.

THE RELEASE

Another extremely important element in the power golf swing is that of release. What does *release* mean? Webster's Dictionary tells us it means "to set free, to let go." Though Webster didn't teach golf, his definition applies. How many times have we hit a golf shot leaving it short and right by "holding on" when we should have "let 'er go" or made a proper release?

Before we consider how a golfer achieves proper release in his golf swing, I would like you to consider some mental pictures of other action sports. These are a few ideas that will help you understand the feeling of release you must have in your golf swing.

First, I would like you to visualize, in your mind's eye, an Olympic champion discus-thrower. See the whole scene, the tremendous crowd in the stadium with all eyes focused on a magnificent athlete as he begins his throw. His right hand is cupped around the outer edge of the 4½-pound disc. He starts from a stationary position and begins to twirl his body counterclockwise with his arm extended, outstretched holding the disc. He whirls faster and faster and then at the precise moment he whirls the metal plate as far as he can.

I want you to imagine yourself flinging the discus. Feel the freedom of the release as the imaginary disc leaves your hand. Feel the acceleration that your body has built up before you let

Players who squeeze the club too tightly will benefit from the feeling of winding up and throwing the club to get a better feeling of release.

the plate go. Then, finally, feel the full extension and releasing rather than tightening.

If you cannot picture yourself as a discus thrower, then try the mental picture of using a slingshot. Hold the imaginary "Y" out in front of you at arm's length and draw back the rubber sling. Put an imaginary golf ball in the sling. Now that the slingshot is at full extension, open your fingers and let it go. Again, you have a fine example of release, the sort of release you must have in your power golf swing.

Relevant to these imaginary games of release is a training trick a tennis coach used in teaching the great tennis star, Maureen Connolly ("Little Mo"). When Maureen was just starting her career, the coach would take about twenty old tennis rackets and put Maureen at the baseline of the court. Then she would order Maureen to throw the rackets overhand as far as she could. She eventually was able to throw some of them into the back court. The result of this odd exercise was that Maureen learned to sense the proper release in her serve. Furthermore, the release training carried over when she kept the racket in her hand and made her serve. And, of course, we all know that she went on to become a great tennis champion.

This is the "shaking hands" position on the right side of the ball, 90° into the downswing. Notice particularly how my right elbow is tucked against my side. This position will help me to stay "under the ball" and behind it at the moment of truth.

The right hand is shown here in the correct release position of shaking hands when the swing is 90° past ball contact.

Using a weighted training device promotes a stronger, more powerful release.

The result of release in a golf swing is allowing the forearms to roll over 180° while keeping their same basic relationship to the body as it turns through. Your right hand will reach a shaking-hands position on each side of your body.

You may have seen a karate expert smash down into a pile of concrete blocks and break them in two. When he performs this remarkable feat, he is not smashing the bricks but using his force of *ki* to move his hand and arm through the blocks to a point beyond that of first impact.

This is an important idea I would like you to consider adopting. Let the golf ball be the karate expert's block of concrete. See your target as a spot somewhere beyond, even down the fairway 225 yards away. You are going to swing *through* the golf ball, not *at* it.

THE FOLLOW-THROUGH

The final stage of the swing, the movement of the clubhead through the ball, happens so quickly that it is impossible for the human eye to follow it. How do we know whether the swing has been executed properly?

There are ways to tell. First, we know by the sound and flight of the ball whether or not it has been well struck. Did the ball leap off the face, find its trajectory quickly and just seem to keep going? If the drive starts low and then continues to climb steeply, you've hit a *riser*. They look good but don't really go anywhere. It's caused by too much clubhead descent rather than a solid forward contact against the back of the ball. We can also tell a great deal by the sound of the shot as it comes off the face of the driver. There is an unmistakable crack to a well-struck drive. You know it, and so do your opponents.

But one of the best ways to tell whether the swing has been a good one is by watching the position of the body in the follow-through. A good follow-through is always the product of a good swing. A bad swing will produce an unbalanced or incomplete follow-through.

Let's define *follow-through* as it is generally understood in golf instruction. It is the position of the hands, arms, and body that is caused by the momentum of the club after the ball has been struck. In a good swing from an inside to on-line path, the clubhead attempts to go out after the ball but in actuality cannot do so because the right hand hangs onto it. So, the clubhead goes up and around the golfer's body. In a truly full follow-through after a good shot the club can often be seen all the way around behind the player's body.

Here's the picture of a full follow-through. The player's

A strong finish is the result of a strong, tension-free swing.

weight has shifted entirely to the left side of his body and is focused over the heel and ball area of the outside of the left foot. Only the inside edge or toe of the right foot remains on the ground. The hips have turned until they are facing the target. The left arm, straight until the *moment of truth* at the bottom of the arc, is now bent and has folded so that the left elbow points toward the ground. The right hand and arm are extended and are rather high. The back of the left hand may be in line with the forearm in much the same relationship the hand and forearm had at the top of the backswing, although many players let the left wrist cup a bit more as they relax at the finish.

If there are flaws in the swing, they will immediately show up in an awkward follow-through. A prematurely released swing from the outside leaves the golfer with much of his weight still on the right side. The golfer's hands will be low and around his body, even below his shoulders. The right knee is apt to be pointing straight out at the ball's original position instead of being well past it as it should be in a good swing. We all can recognize a bad swing just as readily as we recognize and admire a good swing. The trick is how to do it.

One way is to think *finish*. I'll frequently have my pupils "start at the finish." In this drill, they make a relaxed swing to a good finish position. I frequently will make adjustments. They hold that position for 15 seconds, then swing the club to the top of the backswing and return with speed to the finish. This takes their minds off the ball and focuses their attention on a point well past the ball, helping them to maintain clubhead speed through the hitting. The result is more distance.

THE SQUARELY HIT BALL

In striving for distance off the tee, many golfers fail to realize how important it is to strike the ball squarely. As you will discover in the discussion on the mechanical driving machine, a golf ball struck only ½ inch off the face of the clubhead may lose from 10 to as much as 15 percent of its distance.

It is apparent from watching players on the first tee that many

This photo shows a ball being hit near the heel of the club. Any off-center hit will cause loss of distance of up to 20 percent of potential.

Hitting the ball toward the toe of the club also causes serious loss of distance.

golfers believe they can consistently swing with more effort than they should and still hit the ball squarely with good clubhead speed. Often they accomplish neither result. The ball does not go far, and it doesn't go straight because they have swung *too hard*—with too much physical effort. When the ordinary golfer tries to slug the ball, he usually swings too fast on his backswing and produces any one of several actions that actually hinder the momentum of the clubhead and prevent it from reaching maximum acceleration at impact. Some of these faults are: *tightening of the grip,* with the result that the muscles of the forearm are also tightened and not free to produce the maximum clubhead speed; *a fast backswing,* which builds up momentum quickly where at the top of the swing the force of that momentum puts too much strain on the grip. The consequence is either too much tension or loss of the grip at the top, causing a regripping on the way down. This results in an ineffectual, poorly timed, and less effective swing—*too short a backswing,* which is often the result of a "rush for power." Attempting to hit harder is equated with faster and faster turns into shorter which is a definite power loss.

The golfer must not overcontrol the clubhead at any point in his swing. The result is one you've seen so often in fellow players. It looks like they are trying to shove or push the club toward the ball. Overcontrol comes from trying to *make a golf shot* rather than letting a golf swing happen and a shot result. Overcontrol comes from trying to guide the motion rather than freewheeling it. We check that with students by testing their clubhead speeds as they employ various levels of tension and effort.

Dawson prepares to hit a tee shot using a swing analyzer.

Dawson and I analyze the results of his swing on the swing analyzer.

You must realize that the clubface is large enough to allow for considerable error and still hit the ball. As you practice more and more on standardizing your swing, making it repeat the same path over and over again, you will also come to realize that you are not only striking the ball on the clubface but also are striking it more frequently on the "sweet spot" of the face that gives you the most effective power.

When that happens, developing your ability to hit the ball squarely time after time, there will come a new realization that *square hitting* of the golf ball results from a swing that is free from tension and overcontrol. It is imperative that every golfer *swing within himself,* that is, not attempt to produce any more power than the power that results from his basic personal, uninhibited, full-motion effort without any conscious effort to either overcontrol or force the clubhead.

A wonderful thing happens when you stop trying to slug the ball. Concentrating on merely making solid, center-of-the-face freewheeling contact with a rhythmical swing will actually add distance to your shots. You will hit the ball squarely more often than before and thus you will get more clubhead mass behind the ball on more of your shots.

This was well demonstrated to me personally last year on my 381-yard long drive contest effort. That shot happened to be the very first one of the competition, my first of six balls. After being announced, I approached the ball and said to myself, "Now, just swing it freely, hit it solidly, and get it inside the boundaries as a measurable shot. Then you can go after one harder." Well, the easy swing hit it 381, and the next five hard swings snap-hooked it once, popped it up twice, and then sliced it out-of-bounds twice. Don't try to slug the ball. Freewheeling full motion will produce less tension, get greater clubhead speed, and let you finish on balance.

Maintaining balance was one of legendary Sam Snead's greatest assets. How was he able to do that so consistently shot after shot? Because he swung within his controllable power limit rather than beyond it. He found an effective swing speed and didn't try to exceed it. Paul Runyan says, "I've played with and watched Sam Snead hit thousands of shots under all types of conditions for fifty years, and I can only remember him swinging too hard at a shot where he lost his balance on two, maybe three, occasions. That is quite a feat!"

When Snead did go for the "big tee ball," his approach was interesting. He said that he "slowed down," so he would get a bigger, longer turn and create more potential for distance.

It has often been said that no golfer should exert any more than 90 percent of his potential power. I don't know if you could put an accurate percentage on it but you should feel that you have a little extra in reserve. It is difficult sometimes to do that. I know it is for me. But if you can keep some small feeling of reserve strength back you will find that you are not only consistently longer and more accurate but you have an additional psychological edge. You will feel confident, as if you're in control of your swing, not the swing in control of you.

Dr. Cary Middlecoff

"When you face a tough shot in a tight situation, don't get overconcerned with the fact that you might miss it. Hit the shot to the best of your ability and let it go at that. The same attitude is a prerequisite for hitting the long ball."

3
TRAINING AND EXERCISES
MY PERSONAL TRAINING PROGRAM

How fit do you have to be to play golf well? More so than you'd think. Physical deterioration or general lack of conditioning is the number one factor that causes the adult handicap to go up. If your handicap was at one time lower than it is now and you are still playing as frequently as you did before, look to your body first for the answer. Loss of strength and flexibility will alter technique. When your hands and forearms lose strength or suppleness and your straight ball turns into a slice, you automatically start to make adjustments in your aim, grip, and swing path. What you should be doing is conditioning your body.

Don't be fooled when you see a few potbellies on television golf. Most of the PGA Tour players are pretty fair athletes with a high degree of strength and flexibility related to their sport. Even those sporting a portion of their midsection outside their trousers have strong arms, hands, and trunks with more than adequate flexibility. More Tour players are fit than not. Physical training for golf is slowly being recognized on the tour as an important factor in maintaining playing ability. The potential gains for any player are relative to the present condition of the body. The tour players are already reasonably fit because they walk the golf course every day and exercise by hitting many balls. The weekend golfer generally is not. The improvement in performance as a result of training for the player in poor physical condition, particularly the seniors and especially the senior women, would be quite significant.

Let's be honest. No one person has developed, tested, and conclusively demonstrated that his system was the best for developing distance in all physical types. Claims may be made to this effect, but the fact is that the same prescription does not work for everybody. For example, a senior player may have above-average strength but be badly lacking in flexibility. Conversely a female player may possess extreme flexibility but be lacking in strength. Each needs a training program geared to his or her weakness. Training to improve physical deficiencies as well as those in the swing will be an important part of the serious golfer's future.

I'd like to share some training thoughts based on my experience, observation, and experimentation. I certainly don't claim this is the only training program for everyone; but for my objectives of hitting the ball longer, developing better swing technique, and acquiring sufficient endurance to play on successive days in a tournament without undue fatigue, it works.

Strength

What do I do for strength? First, I want reasonable total body balance with special emphasis on fingers, hands, back, trunk, and legs. My primary strength building system is based on progressive weight training using Nautilus equipment, although another system like Universal or free weights can also be used. The reason I've chosen Nautilus is that it's convenient for me, it's based on sound principles of progressive resistance, the machines allow me to isolate specific muscle groups, and the equipment is comfortable and relatively safe. There may be

Charlotte McGinnis is a strong woman, able to hold two irons at arm's length in her left hand. Strength is a factor in club control and in distance.

Lack of strength to hold two clubs at arm's length horizontal with the ground is quite common among female players and demonstrates an important causal relationship with lack of distance.

better training regimes for golf, but Nautilus is so widely accepted and distributed that for most people, the equipment is accessible in their communities.

I also use secondary strength developers such as "The Distance Builder" swing device, "Gym-in-a-Bag" home and travel kit, "The Grip," and a few calisthenics that I'll discuss later. If I dropped Nautilus and used these secondary developers exclusively, I could still create an excellent workout.

To develop strength you need overload. Overload makes your muscles do more work than that to which they are accustomed. You accomplish this by increasing either the load lifted or the number of times you lift it. An example would be to load a barbell with the amount of weight you can press over your head eight times consecutively. Do that on Monday, then nine times on Wednesday, and ten times on Friday. On the following Monday, add five pounds and go back to eight repetitions. That's overload. The body needs the in-between days for resting and rebuilding the muscle tissue. Light daily workouts are possible and may be effective for the golfer, but the pros with the greatest strength who work out vigorously need rest days. One workout per week for the trained athlete is not enough to maintain his fitness level. For the untrained—the person who does little or nothing—it will improve his condition up to a point. Two days a week can definitely improve your condition; three times a week is the most beneficial because your effort does not have to be terribly intense, and you still are giving the body a day off.

Intensity is something you must treat very carefully. Frankly, my biggest weakness is working out too hard before I'm adequately trained, causing either over-fatigue or injury. Train, don't strain. If you are out of condition and it has taken twenty years to get that way, don't try to reverse your condition in two weeks or you'll likely become an exercise dropout. Your anticipated feeling of dynamic health will turn into one of fatigue and soreness, the by-products of doing too much, too soon.

Exercising regularly is far more important than achieving big increases in the amount of weights you lift. On Nautilus equipment, for example, the plates are loaded in ten-pound increments. For most of your golf exercises, increases should be undertaken in five pound or two-and-a-half pound increments. This is made possible on Nautilus by using loose plates which are available at any center.

When I'm not on the road, a workout week would look something like this:

Monday
Morning—stretching and routine exercises, 10 minutes.
Afternoon (either at lunch-time or after work)—Nautilus workout including Distance Builder swings, Sit-ups, and flexibility work. Total time: 30–40 minutes.

Tuesday
Morning—jog and stretching; Gym-in-a-Bag power pull, and Sit-ups.

Wednesday
Same as Monday.

Thursday
Same as Tuesday.

Friday
Same as Monday. Sometimes I skip Friday and do my Nautilus on Saturday.
If Nautilus is done on Saturday, then I run Sunday.

Saturday
Same as Thursday, although my run is more often in the afternoon or evening, as I play golf Saturday morning.

Sunday
Rest. Sometimes a short jog and Sit-ups.

This workout schedule is light to moderate for an athlete in training but somewhat ambitious for the busy working person with a family who is trying to get in some golf time. However, it can be done if you eliminate most of the television watching and are willing to get up a little earlier in the day.

The Nautilus® Workout

The use of Nautilus training has swept the country, its equipment and systems dominating spas and workout centers. Understand that there is no magic in Nautilus equipment; it is simply effective in developing strength, maintaining flexibility, and, in some instances, aiding cardiovascular fitness. But *you* still have to produce the physical work.

The Nautilus gospel (as preached by self-styled fitness guru Arthur Jones) is that muscular balance is the answer to improvement in all sports. Students are therefore encouraged to perform the whole line of exercises with little attention paid to specificity of sport. I do not disagree with that concept for general health and fitness, but I do disagree if you want to swing a golf club effectively.

A certain percentage of the population is so poorly conditioned that any exercise would help them regardless of their sport. In a finely tuned skill activity like golf, in which a certain pattern or sequence of motion is critical, it's different. That is why I'm advocating that the use of Nautilus or any weight-training system be limited to certain exercises, depending upon your needs.

There are some exercises to shun and others to do with guarded enthusiasm. If you feel that you are really out of shape, go ahead and do the regular program. But if you already have a modest level of fitness, I would consider the following recommendations:

1. *Biceps Curls,* even though practiced through a full range of motion, will tend to shorten your arc length in the golf swing. There is no move in golf which resembles the biceps curl unless it is a counterproductive move. *Stay away from the Biceps Curl.*

2. *The Triceps Press* can have some value particularly if the emphasis is on your left arm. The left tricep does play a role in pulling the arm toward the target and both the right and left in arm extension. However, developing bulk in the triceps can inhibit the pattern of your arm swing across your chest. Do this exercise with caution, and watch out that you don't build bulk.

3. *The Chest* or *Bench Press* is definitely a bad exercise for golfers, since the larger the pectoral muscles in the chest become, the farther the arms must swing away from the body. Though the pectorals do contract in the golf swing, they contribute little to the force of the swing. Conversely, if the pectorals are well-developed, they can definitely detract from the desired technique.

4. *Military Press* or *Arm Press* is a deltoid (shoulder) developer, which enhances movements which are not of particular value to the golfer. In fact, you must be very careful not to inhibit the suppleness of the shoulder girdle and fluidity of the arm swing. Powerful deltoids pull the golfer's shoulders back: a classic position for the sculptured body of a gymnast or body builder but a detriment to the golfer. Give me the round-shouldered athlete with muscles bulging in his back, not his front.

We've dwelled on the negative; what about the positive? What *should* you do?

The machines at Nautilus that I use are listed in the order in which I use them:

1. *Hip and Back*—Until the facility where I work out acquires a *back extension machine,* I've reduced the loads on the hip and back to 75 percent of my maximum (just to play safe)

The hip and back Nautilus machine. Be careful to see that you are strapped in tightly so there is no arching of your lower back.

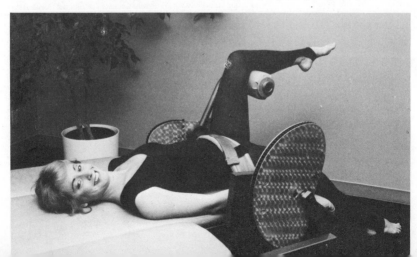

since I was getting severe soreness and some pain in the lower back when I worked at maximum levels.

2. *Leg Extension*—This muscle group is a weakness of mine since I had knee injuries from college football and knee surgery

Leg Extensions help in the development of the muscles and ligament and tendon structure surrounding the knee joint. They help provide the golfer with better stability.

five years ago. For that reason, I work hard on this exercise although I don't rate it as high for golfers in general as several other exercises. The free weight equivalent of this exercise is sitting on a table and extending your leg with a weighted boot on your foot.

3. *Leg Press*—Here is an important exercise for almost every sport. The free weight equivalent is a half squat (never full) with a barbell on the shoulders.

4. *Leg Curls*—This is basically a leg exercise for the hamstrings, but takes on added importance for golf because of its work on the buttocks and lower back.

5. *Pullover*—The latissimus dorsi muscles are the large muscles in the back which run from under the arm up to the level of the shoulders and across the back to the spine. They are

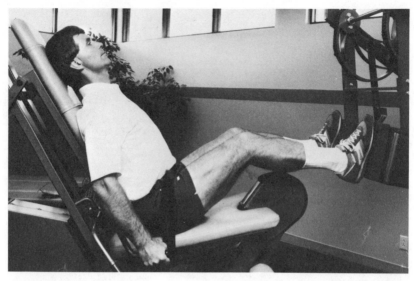

Leg Presses develop the quadriceps, the largest muscle group in your legs.

Leg Curls for the hamstring, gluteus, and lower back

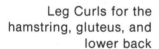

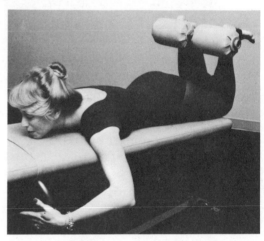

contributors to the series of link actions that make up the golf swing. A free weight exercise for these muscles is the two-arm pullover in which you lift a barbell over your head while lying on your back. The range of motion is much greater with Nautilus. Use light weights only if you are large in the upper body.

6. *Rowing*—Again, this will strengthen the muscles of the back without producing unnecessary shoulder and chest development. A free weight exercise could be done using a barbell, pulling it to the chest while standing bent forward 90° from the waist.

7. *Adductor-Abductor*—This is a good golf exercise for the inner and outer leg. Weighted boots are needed in a free weight system as you lie on your side and elevate your upper leg for a positive abduction and then resistance or gravity for a negative pull to get the adduction.

8. *Abdominal*—The muscles of the stomach are important for posture and for helping to prevent low back pain. The center of the body is also an important part of your power link system. The Nautilus abdominal machine works this area. With free weights, use weight plates held behind your head and do bent knee sit-ups (curl-ups) with feet braced. Never do sit-ups with the knees flat on the floor. Try to find the new abdominal machine.

The abdominal muscles, another important muscle group for golf power, are being worked here.

The rotary torso machine provides one of the best exercises for golf.

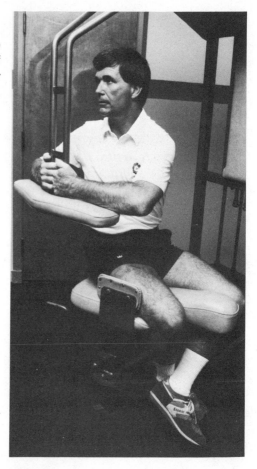

9. *Rotary Torso*—An exercise unique to Nautilus equipment and particularly good for the golfer, this strengthens and stretches the muscles that rotate the torso and are so much a part of the golf swing. It is difficult to find a counterpart in free weight exercise. We modify by gripping from under, rather than over, the pad.

10. *Triceps Press*—You want strong (but not large) triceps. This machine helps develop the muscles to stabilize the left arm as it pulls in horizontal extension and gives extension to both arms. The equivalent in free weights is a *triceps press* with barbell or dumbbells.

Toe Raises build the calf or gastrocnemius muscles, an important group for golf.

11. *Rise on Toes*—This is done on the multi-machine with a belt and is for the *calf* or *gastrocnemius muscles.* It may be performed with free weights by holding a barbell across your shoulders while you raise and lower yourself on your toes.

12. *Side Bends*—Again, do this on the multi-machine, with a hand strap alternating between the right and left side. A similar exercise with free weights is performed using a barbell across the shoulders.

Above all else, work on exercising your back, particularly the lower back. Nautilus users should work on the *back extension machine,* perhaps the best piece of equipment the company has ever made. Unfortunately, it's a latecomer to the line and only a small percentage of Nautilus Fitness Centers have them. Although the standard *hip and back machine* is a substitute, it's one that I feel requires great caution. Since the *hip and back machine* allows your back to arch off the pad (even when you are strapped down), it puts tremendous pressure on your lower back and can cause strains when you are working near your maximum. Be extra cautious—bad backs have shortened more golf careers than any other injury. The muscles of the lower back are important in helping prevent poor posture, leading to disc and nerve problems. The stress loads placed on the back in a vigorous, athletic golf swing are substantial. If you are in pain and can't use your back muscles properly, you have lost a powerful element in your link action system.

The Distance Builder*

Players have been encouraged for years to swing a weighted club to develop stronger golf muscles. I've received reports from several players who say they have profited from this experience. However, not all bio-mechanics scholars would agree that it will increase your swing speed. In fact, some would contend that it interferes with technique.

My personal feeling is that this latter theory might be true at the highest levels of performance, during their season, but the benefits of strength and flexibility gained by the multitude of golfers who need those qualities far offset any interference with their technique. In fact, the added strength and flexibility would afford most of them an improved technique.

The Distance Builder incorporates progressive resistance exercise and can be a key to a home training program.

Distance Builder may be ordered by writing to the following address:

Mr. Bill Wendt
HAPPE Products (W)
712 South Oak Avenue
Marshfield, WI 54449

To strengthen the forearms rotate the Distance Builder or weighed club 180°.

Repeat 8–10 times, over and back, with each arm. Grip higher or lower to change resistance or you may add more weight.

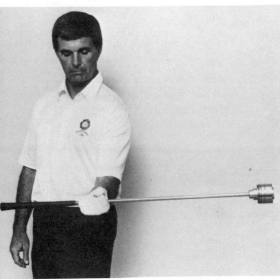

Full swing drill from the top. . . .

. . . Retaining the hit . . .

. . . Stress square contact
with the back of the left wrist
flat at impact . . .

. . . then releasing to the . . .

. . . finish.

Hold the club alternately in the left then the right hand behind the back, pulling down with the opposite hand for a strong stretch.

Perform this gravity drill to feel weight over right leg; then step and swing, letting the weight shift help pull your arms through.

A good starting drill with abbreviated swing traveling 180° in the impact area from the right hip to the left hip. This is called the "shake hands" exercise.

Shaking hands with the right on the other side of the body to finish the 180° move.

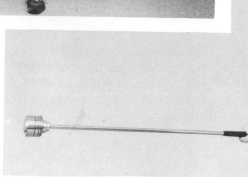

Start with the weighted club horizontal to the ground out in front of you, elbows in.

Cock the club over each shoulder while keeping the left wrist flat.

Lower the club to the starting
position, then cock the wrists
so that the club goes over the
right shoulder.

The Distance Builder is a golf club-like apparatus which progressively adds resistance in the form of weighted rings. As the golfer grows stronger, he or she adds another ring. I swing it for three sets of twelve repetitions, with thirty-second rest intervals between each set. Every other session, I add one ounce of weight. I try to swing my best full driver swing—with as close to perfect form as possible—and I stop adding weights or, if necessary, take off weights whenever my form starts to deteriorate.

After the three sets with the Distance Builder, I take a driver and swing for speed. Then I use a shaft that is gripped but has no clubhead and I swing it for speed, emphasizing good form, a feeling of free-wheeling, and an uninhibited swinging motion. That comprises a Nautilus workout day as I end with golf swings.

If you do not have weight training facilities of any kind readily available, using the Distance Builder alone can have a surprising benefit. There are also several exercises you can do besides simply swinging the Distance Builder. I've worked up a series which includes pronation-supination, 30-second slow motion swing, triceps-pull-behind-the-back, step and swing, 180° drill, and over-the-shoulder-wrist-cocking.

Gym-in-a-Bag*

Here is an exercise device that is simple, inexpensive, portable, and effective. When I don't have access to other equipment, this is my means of getting a resistance workout. When I'm at home, on a regular routine, I only use it for supplemental to two exercises in the morning. I first hook the strap in the door just below shoulder height and close the door to provide the resistance. Putting my left arm across my chest, I reach back and grab hold of a strap as though it were a grip on the club halfway into

Using Gym-in-a-Bag, pull with the left side to the impact area, releasing tension on the rope with the right hand. Repeat five times.

the downswing. Pulling against this resistance, I gradually release tension with the right hand until I pull past the hitting area. I then turn my body 180° and face the opposite direction, take the strap in my left palm, and with that arm extended reverse the direction of the pull. The move is similar to a left-handed, forehand tennis stroke. This exercise helps develop the

Gym-in-a-Bag may be ordered by writing to the following address:
Gym-in-a-Bag Products
Box 12535G
Lake Park, FL 33403

Start erect with your left hand in the strap of Gym-in-a-Bag and your right hand controlling the tension.

Full flexion for the abdominals

strength to brake the left arm in the forward swing, and to let the club catch up in whiplike fashion at the ball. Next I put my right elbow near my right pocket, reach back and grab a strap to pull against the resistance of my left until my right palm gets just past the club-ball contact position. Other exercises are possible as well.

TRAINING AT HOME OR OFFICE

There never seems to be enough time to get everything done. Our good intentions so often fall short of fulfillment. We are always going to—practice the piano, work on our German vocab, read the latest best seller, run three miles, write those overdue letters, hit golf balls, do our exercises. But the day passes and today's goal becomes tomorrow's promise. Worse yet, "one of these days I'm going to" eventually becomes "none of these days," and the dreams of accomplishment fade as we realize the time is gone irrevocably. That doesn't have to happen if you learn to build in the practice time toward your goal as a habit each day in your life.

Other Exercises

Here are some very important stretching and isometric exercises you can do at home every day. The two warm-ups pictured below are essential pre-game exercises.

Pictured at left is one of the best stretching exercises to loosen back and shoulder muscles.

It's important to warm up the lower back muscles. Place the club in your elbow joints behind your back and make your swing. Do six swings.

A few years ago, I did a feature in *Golf Digest* that I called "Bathroom Exercises." These are exercises that you can associate with some other habitual activity and build into your daily routine. For example, you can do Sit-ups during television commercial breaks, or use a grip squeezer or rubber bands at your desk or in the front seat of the car. The "bathroom exercises" go like this:

BATHROOM EXERCISES

DAILY ACTIVITY	EXERCISE ATTACHED TO DAILY ACTIVITY
Turn on the shower water and let it get hot.	Neck rolls and side bend stretching, fingers laced over head.
Turn on water for wash basin, let it get hot and fill up.	Lace fingers behind back and swing head down to touch nose to knees. Force arms upward.
Wash and lather for shave.	Rise on toes.
Shave.	Continue rise on toes, some one-legged, plus isometric tummy tighteners.
Brush teeth.	Two-legged, or one-legged, Half-Knee Bends or Squats.
Put on deodorant.	Achilles stretch, reach to ceiling.
Comb hair, use after-shave.	Tighten middle region of body—stomach, buttocks, and upper thighs—with strong isometrics.
Leave bathroom.	Stand in doorway and do isometrics.

This is almost a daily ritual (no one is 100 percent). It's not much—but it is something. If I get shut out from the rest of my normal routine because of an impossible schedule, at least I've gotten in my bathroom exercises.

Occasionally I swim, which I think is productive in helping a golfer loosen and relax his body. Bicycling would be my first substitute for jogging if I ever got up enough motivation to trade in my auto ride for a bike ride to work and back.

Jogging is a part of my program although I am only a casual jogger, going about six to ten miles per week. I'm not training

An isometric exercise to firm the left side and trunk. Hold for 10 seconds but continue normal breathing. Try to keep the right elbow just ahead of the right hand.

The finger pull and any other finger strengthening exercises are valuable to the golfer.

to run. I'm training to finish a golf round without undue fatigue and simply to feel better for anything I do in life.

But built-ins are a blessing for the busy, motivated person. Let's take your mental and physical training for golf as an example. Think of some things you do every working day and attach a built-in activity to it. When you roll out of bed, how about rolling right onto the floor and doing those stretching exercises on page 68? Or, why not build in the bathroom exercises? If yours is normally the coffeepot and TV routine, make the television watching time productive. I've done situps to Jane Pauley's sweet smile on NBC for several years. The jog before breakfast—and for me before TV—is a Tuesday, Thursday, and weekend ritual. It's no big thing—a couple of miles—but it's regular. It raises my pulse to between 130–150 beats per minute, where I want it to be for cardiovascular improvement. I'm training to finish strong on the 17th and 18th holes, not to compete in the latest marathon run in my neighborhood.

How do you get to work? Can you ride your bike? Can you walk? Either could have a fitness component built in. Like most people I drive to work, but on the dashboard of my car is a grip squeezer and rubber bands. Forearm flexor and extensor muscle

These sit on the dashboard of my car. The squeezer is for flexion; the rubber bands are for extension.

It's not easy to find an apparatus that works your extensors. Rubber bands are quite simple.

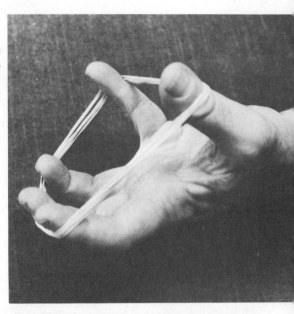

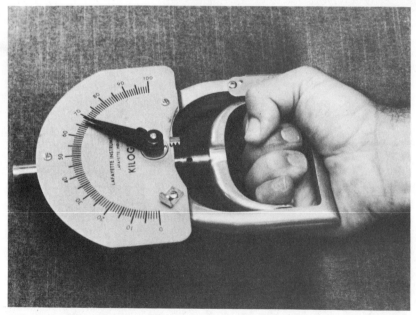

A grip manuometer measures grip strength, a good measure of overall body strength. You need strength here for club control, not just distance.

exercises are built in as I simultaneously work on another part of my training—the mental part. Sitting beside me is a cassette tape recorder and some of the best speakers and motivators in the world. They are all available on audiocassette. The most complete selection of speakers to shape your attitude for positive, aggressive, winning golf comes from the Nightingale-Conant Corporation.* Although the subject may not be specifically golf, the pattern and formula for success is much the same in all activities. It centers around confidence, mental toughness, perseverance, a positive attitude, imaging success, and the ability to relax.

So built into my ride to the office is a short but regular practice period. Personally I find this one of the greatest sources of built-in benefit, all because of the availability of a couple of simple strength gadgets and an inexpensive tape player and some great people to listen to. On the other hand, that same drive to work could add up to a lot of wasted time. That's your choice.

The office where I work has an elevator. I never use it. I've watched too many secretaries with nice figures get chained to a desk, take two coffee breaks and a lunch each day, eat doughnuts and cake every time there is a birthday in the office, plus regularly ride the elevator. It takes about three years to see the spread set in, but it's inevitable and uncomplimentary. Climbing the stairs would at least help the legs. In golf when you lose your legs you lose your platform, your base, your source of stability. Riding in elevators and golf carts won't help.

Office work is sedentary. It's tough to be an athlete, a golfing athlete, when the exercise in your job consists of lifting mortgages, running up quotas, balancing ledgers, pushing sales, or pulling some strings. I'm lucky. The closest workout facility, a Nautilus Center at PGA National, is only a few minutes away. I seldom eat lunch away from the office. Most of the time it's a yogurt or a light sandwich at my desk. But on Monday, Wednesday, and Friday I take what time I'd spend on lunch

---

*Nightingale-Conant Corporation, 3730 West Devon Avenue, Chicago, Illinois, also carries video and audio cassettes of "The Greater Golfer in You" by Gary Wiren.

away to get in a 30-minute workout on the exercise machines followed by a short relaxing swim. Time away from desk: one hour. On the weekend, I focus more on my golf and run.

Priorities

If it's strictly golf improvement you are after and your time is limited on how much you can do, I'd choose the following activities in order of their contribution to golf improvement for most people.

1. Take instruction and hit balls on the range.
2. Play golf.
3. Practice swinging—doing drills—visualizing and feeling swing.
4. Exercises related to golf strength and, more important for me, flexibility: Nautilus, Distance Builder, Gym-in-a-Bag, stretching series.
5. Jog, bicycle, swim, or built-in exercises.

If you can do all these things, it's that much better. We have given considerable space to the development of strength. But you must understand that flexibility is more important for distance than people realize. The primary cause of decreased distance is the loss of range of motion or flexibility, *not* loss of strength. Obviously, both take place as we age. However, restricted motion leads more to a poor technique than does restricted strength. And through the link-action system, technique is still the most important factor in producing distance. Therefore, I recommend that you include flexibility exercises, such as some of those contained in basic Hatha yoga to keep your spine, back, shoulders, and trunk as flexible as possible. Those pictured here are very useful for golf.

Developing a good golf swing will bring you as close to your potential distance as any single factor. Specialized training for strength and flexibility, having the right equipment, and having the right state of mind will all enhance your distance produc-

This exercise, elbows together and arms forced upward, is one that is used by long drive champion Terry Forcum.

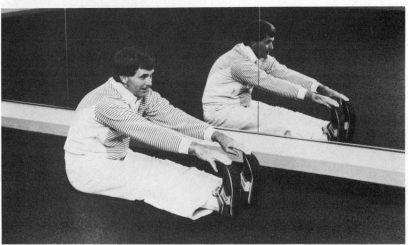

Reach for the toes to stretch the hamstrings in the backs of your legs. Start by grabbing legs at the ankles and then work your way down. Hold 15 seconds and repeat.

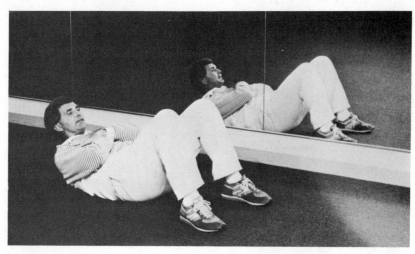

With your feet and back flat against the floor, arms folded across the chest, roll up slowly to a half Sit-up, hold, and then roll down. Do as many as you can without discomfort.

This is a good body stretcher, particularly when you try to arch your head and back backward. Hold for 15 seconds and then switch the leading leg.

Roll up into a tight ball and rock to loosen your trunk, back, and legs. Repeat 15 times.

In a reverse clasp, hold
your arms over your head
and stretch and twist.

With my right hand
reaching down my back, I
push down on the elbow
with the left hand to
increase shoulder
flexibility.

Then reverse. Do for 15 seconds on each side.

This body pivot is great for increasing your backswing length. Keep your feet at a right angle to the wall and flat on the floor. Hold for 30 seconds and then switch directions.

With the soles of your feet together, knees out, grab your feet and tug them toward you for a good stretch on the inside of your legs and ankles.

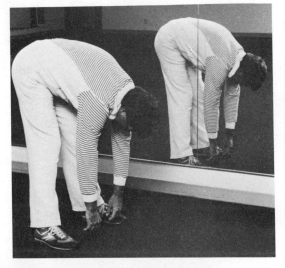

At right: Hang downward with your knees slightly flexed. Let out your breath and hang lower, gradually straightening your legs. Don't bounce. Do for 30 seconds. Below: This is a "leg over" in one direction with the trunk rotated in the other direction. Hold for 15 seconds and reverse.

Clasp hands, bend to the side in line with your body. Gradually increase the bend and hold that position. Do 30 seconds on each side.

tion, but in smaller increments. The only exceptions to that are people in such poor physical condition that for them swinging a golf club properly is out of the question until their body is fit enough to do it. That includes a lot of golfers.

GARY WIREN'S PERSONAL TRAINING PROGRAM

STRENGTH EXERCISES: 3 days/week

NAUTILUS
1. Back Extension—or Hip and Back Machine if Back Extension not available
2. Rotary Torso
3. Leg Extension
4. Leg Press
5. Leg Curl

6. Rise on Toes (also do a set of Half Squats with same load)
7. Side Bends
8. Abdominal
9. Triceps Press
10. Ad-Ab

POWER BUILDER

1. 180° Flat Wrist (Stretching: Behind Back—Low)
2. Pronator-Supinator, Right and Left (Stretching: Behind Back, High Extension)
3. Step and Swing (Stretching: Triceps Stretch)
4. Slo-Mo-Swing (Stretching: Side Bend Stretch)
5. Regular Swing (Stretching: Forward Flex)
6. Swing for Speed Regular Club (Light Club—Matzie)

FLEXIBILITY EXERCISES

1. Salute the Sun
2. Golf series

CARDIO-VASCULAR EXERCISES

1. Jogging—2 miles 3 times/week— *or* 3 miles 2 times/week
2. Swimming
3. Bicycling

GENERAL EXERCISES

1. Sit-ups
2. Back exercises

BUILT-IN EXERCISES

1. Squeeze ball or grip device
2. Rubber bands

ON THE ROAD

1. "Gym in a Bag"
2. Jogging or Stair Climbing

HAND AND ARM STRENGTH

In a test conducted on a mechanical ball-hitting machine, modifications were made to create a more humanlike result. Instead of gripping the club in its usual viselike fashion, the investigators were allowed to put sponge rubber around the grip much like the fleshy pad of the hand. In addition, the pressure applied by the clamps was similar to that exerted by a human hand. The purpose of the test was to compare the results of off-center hits when gripped in the normal viselike fashion versus the more human softer method. "Sweet spot" hits traveled relatively the same distance; but in the off-center hits, the human softer grip produced far more dispersion and deviation from straight than the firmly clamped shots.

Tight gripping by the player is not the answer, but a firm yet relaxed grip is. Tightness doesn't work because it restricts the action in your forearms and wrist, producing a stiff-looking and slow-moving clubhead. You need strength in your arms and hands for firmness and to be able to accomplish it by gripping lightly, not tightly. If you are strong, you can control the club without exerting great tension in your hands and arms.

A great example of the importance of hand and arm strength was Ben Hogan who was asked how many perfect full shots he had hit when he set the record of 276 strokes in the U.S. Open at Riviera Country Club in 1948. Ben replied, "Not more than a dozen."

The conclusion might be that even the great Hogan suffered off-center hits a fair share of the time. But because Ben had extremely strong hands and arms, his off-center shots were not deflected as much as they are in the case of the ordinary golfer with considerably weaker hands and arms. Hogan's statement lends even more authority to my claim that in order to drive the ball farther and straighter you must strengthen your hands and arms by systematic exercise.

THE MIND AS WELL AS THE BODY

Does the mind really affect long driving, or is long driving strictly in the domain of the physical and mechanical? You can easily answer that by attending any athletic event where the performer is attempting to produce a maximum physical effort such as weight-lifting, shot-putting, high jump, the long jump, the pole vault, or other similar track events. In the moments before these sports performances there is inevitably a great deal of self-psyching—using the mind to prepare the body for peak performance. The mind most certainly has an effect. It does in golf as well, but in a different manner. The production of power is not the only issue. Control and consistency must be blended with power. Instead of *psyching up,* in golf the mind is more

The headphones that I'm wearing provide relaxing music from the player attached to my belt in back.

frequently used to *psych down*—or to reduce the tension level. What you want is a high energy level and low tension level, an almost cavalier, "I don't care," such as the Fuzzy Zoeller–Lee Trevino approach to the whole thing where you are enjoying the experience and freewheeling. Tension is the great destroyer of the swing, and without a mechanically effective swing you can't possibly produce your best distance. So tension is a distance killer.

Your body won't lie for your brain. If you are saying to yourself, "This one is going 260 right down the middle . . . 260 . . . 260 . . . ," then when you get to the top of your backswing an inner voice says, "Don't slice it out-of-bounds," you have no chance. Inevitably you'll hit from the top and pull across the ball or tense your body so badly the shot will be *blocked out,* ending up in the very place you were trying to avoid. In any case you'll most certainly not get the kind of surprising distance that comes from a more relaxed freewheeling state of mind. The license to freewheel is issued by the mind. And your mind must be broadcasting positive pictures.

I call it *surprising distance,* because you don't feel as though you are expending a great deal of physical effort. It almost feels like a full motion practice swing. Let me give you an example. I had a student who could make a 2 handicap practice swing; but when the ball was put down in front of him, he barely played to his 18. The smooth-flowing, accelerating, slinging, uninhibited, whistling motion when his target was only air turned into a jerky, abbreviated, slashing, tension-filled lunge when the ball was placed in the way. Obviously the rest of the problem was not physical or mechanical. This golfer had all the strength, flexibility, and technique needed. Without them he couldn't have produced such a beautiful practice effort. What was keeping him from repeating that swing was the sight of the ball. We tried everything. "Pretend it's a soap bubble." "Hit it with your practice swing." "Swing through, not at." "Close your eyes," and the teacher's last-straw comment: "Just relax." The advice was to no avail. The pattern persisted: well-paced fluid practice swings *through* to the target . . . followed by disaster—a muscularly tight forced hit *at* the ball. One evening while at home my cerebral light went on. I had remembered reading of a plausible solution—a trick. The next day I bought a half dozen plastic balls, ones with solid exteriors, no holes in them, and I painted them black. I also got a half dozen high compression seconds and painted them black. I called my pupil. When he arrived I showed him the dozen balls, and with a statement of intended deception (much like a carnival sleight of hand expert) said, "Now we have here a dozen black plastic balls." I proceeded to demonstrate with a plastic example that they wouldn't bounce off the concrete higher than my ankle and when struck full force would die at 30 yards. I told him, "Why try to hit hard . . . it won't go anywhere . . . just swing!"

I placed the first black plastic ball on the tee. He looked convinced. Apparently he was, because he put his practice swing motion on the first shot and sailed a beauty out there about 25 yards. Then another and another. "See how easy it is." On the fourth shot I slipped in one of the real balls painted black. It was next to impossible to tell the difference. He swung. You should have seen his face! The most beautiful effortless drive—240 yards—straight as the state lines in Colorado. He had actually hit one with his practice swing. The mind, in this case, just needed to be tricked.

But developing a good golf mind is not just tricks. The mind can also be trained. The training for hitting your longest tee shots requires that you see positive results in order to let you freewheel. Pick an area where you want the ball to go—not some target so precise it tightens you up. Visualize your swing and the flight of the ball, its trajectory and shape. Then rehearse your swing to reinforce freedom of motion and pace—and let it go.

Let me caution you, however, about standing over the shot too long. If you are seeking precise accuracy, a little extra time in your shot routine might be helpful. But if it's your longest distance you are seeking without having the narrow confines of a tight driving area, I'd suggest this little routine that I use for those long par fives that are wide open. Simply incorporate these three words in your preshot routine: *Ready—Aim—Flier.* *Ready* is seeing your visual picture and placing both hands precisely on the grip; *Aim* is getting the clubface and body aimed where you desire; and *Flier* is winding up and letting the clubhead fly toward your target. These are simply thoughts and pictures of the mind, but they have a great deal to do with tension reduction and therefore with distance.

Jack Nicklaus

"... A golfer who learns to swing hard initially can usually acquire accuracy later, whereas a golfer who gets too accuracy conscious at the outset will rarely be able to make himself hit the ball hard later on."

4
EQUIPMENT

A DRIVER THAT FITS YOUR GAME

Your driver is one of the most enticing clubs in your bag. If you have confidence in it, you can't wait to tee up that brand-new golf ball and give it a ride. On the other hand, for many golfers, the driver is an intimidating club. Memories of shots out-of-bounds, of topped or skied drives cause many a golfer to fear his driver. Some golfers even reconcile themselves to the fact that they simply cannot handle the driver. They resort to using a 3-wood and getting less distance off the tee. For a temporary cure that may be smart, but for the long run you are at a distinct disadvantage if you can't use your driver.

Although it may take some searching and some experimenting, you can find a driver that fits your swing. Here are some important checkpoints for you to consider in choosing a suitable, effective driver; one that will help you drive the ball longer and straighter:

1. Shaft flex
2. Shaft length

3. Face angle
4. Loft angle
5. Lie angle
6. Swing weight and overall weight
7. Depth of face
8. Face progression
9. Esthetics—do you like its looks?

The most critical element in your driver is its shaft flex. Since it is the longest club in the bag, it tends to flex more than any other in the swing. In order to check whether you are using the proper shaft flex for you, you must analyze the driving results you are now getting. If you are hitting high hooks most of the time, it could be an indication that your shaft is too flexible for you. If you are hitting low shots to the right with a fade, it is probably a sign that the shaft is too stiff for you.

Here's the Matzie wood club with an extremely flexible shaft. A player who has very low levels of clubhead speed shoud try such a flexible shaft. It can add distance by allowing the clubface to kick in and square up at impact.

High-speed cameras show us that the tip end of the shaft bows forward as it approaches the impact area. Picture the shaft at impact as a gentle curve to the left (for right-handers, of course) from your hand to the ball. The more flex the shaft has the more it will bend. For each half inch the lower end bows forward the clubhead will close approximately two degrees. Obviously the stiffer shaft bows less than the more flexible shaft. That is why golfers who use stiff shafts, if they can control them and get sufficient clubhead speed, have more control and a lower trajectory.

The conventional length of a driver is 43 inches. There is no question that the longer the club, the longer the swing arc. But, the longer the club, the farther the golfer is from the ball. And the farther away the golfer is from his target the more difficult

The length of shaft demonstrated by June George ranges here from 41″ to 47″. The long shaft provides greater leverage but becomes increasingly hard to control.

it is for him to return the clubface to the same place every time and strike the ball on the sweet spot or center of the face. So again, you may have to trade off increased length in your driver for loss of accuracy and solid hitting. I recommend that only the low to middle handicap player use a driver longer than 43 inches. Most golfers with higher handicaps do not have grooved swings and the result for them with a longer driver will be a far larger dispersion pattern and more off-center hits.

The term "face angle" is used to describe the positions of the clubface—square, closed, or open—when the club is seated naturally behind the ball, that is, with no manipulation by the hands of the golfer. Ralph Maltby, famous clubmaker and technical consultant to *Golf Magazine,* claims that in his experience 90 percent of all drivers are built with faces about 2 degrees open. He says, "Consequently the average golfer can't quite figure out why he is hitting the ball to the right off the tee. A fully square face will appear a couple of degrees hooked or closed at address."

It is very important that you know what face angle you have

The design of this metal-head wood is derived from Dr. Joseph Corvi's design to dimple the top of the clubhead in order to create turbulence in the air flow and help break up the drag force.

on your driver. If you are a chronic slicer you should consider using a driver with a slightly closed face. The player with the problem of hooking should consider a driver with a more open face. So, check the face angle of your driver this way. Let it lean against a wall and then stand about six feet away directly opposite the toe of the club. If the toe appears to be laid back, you have an open clubface. If the heel area appears to be behind the toe, the face is closed. Remember, too, that if you are happy with the feel of your driver but believe your face angle is unsuitable for you, a good clubmaker can correct the face angle easily. Sometimes that is the solution to a driver problem instead of going to the expense of a new club. There is something great about the feel of a familiar old driver, too, that can never be replaced no matter how hard you try.

Conventional drivers have 11 degrees of loft. Special drivers are built now with more or less than 11 degrees. Interestingly, Andy Franks, one of the Long Driving champions, uses a driver with 7 degrees of loft. A loft angle of more than 11 degrees produces increased backspin, higher shots, less roll, and less distance. Tom Hardman, of the Wilson staff, claims that experimentation with the mechanical driving machine has proved that the ideal launch angle is 9 degrees in order to achieve the greatest distance in carry and roll. At this angle of launch, the ball will achieve a 45-degree trajectory at its highest point. This 9-degree optimum angle, of course, is established at a fairly high rate of clubhead speed. For short hitters whose balls do not rise because of a lower spin velocity, a more lofted wood may produce greater distance for them.

We must be aware that the actual loft of a driver can be and is changed by the angle of attack on the golf ball. By playing the ball forward an inch or so in the stance, the 11-degree driver could launch a ball at a 13- or 14-degree angle. By playing it back an inch, an 11-degree driver may launch the ball at 9 degrees.

So, if you are driving the ball too low, you might consider a driver with increased loft, 12 or even 13 degrees. If you are hitting your drives too high and losing distance, you might want to change to a club with 9 or 10 degrees of loft.

"Lie angle" refers to the angle the club shaft makes when you are soling it naturally in preparation for your normal swing. When you sole your driver, it should rest on a spot one inch toward the heel of the club. A club that sits too far back on the heel will cause a pull to the left; one that, when soled, rests more toward the toe will cause a push to the right. Of course, too, the way you hold your hands on the club has the final effect on lie angle. Hands held low tip the toe of the club up; hands held high bring the toe down. You must experiment to find the lie angle that suits your swing. Your professional can counsel you and I recommend that you take his advice.

The term "swing weight" refers to the balance of the club in motion and defines the relationship between the shaft and the clubhead. It is measured on an arbitrary scale with band C being light, D heavier, and E the heaviest. The physical laws involved when you apply this to a club in motion are complicated. Suffice it to say that as a general rule a driver that is heavier in swing weight or total weight, or both, will tend to cause the golfer to lose clubhead speed and thus lose distance as well. Yet an unusually light driver can cause you to be too quick and can be hard to control. The feather-light clubs will add distance to the shots of most golfers. But a very few players may be seeking consistent accuracy *more* than added distance. Frank Sauchak, brother of the all-time record score holder in a PGA event, used to drive farthest with a club that had an E-9 swingweight. Once again, it is one of those situations in which you must experiment for yourself to find the swing weight and overall weight that gives you the best control and the best results.

"Face depth" refers to the distance between the sole and the top of the face of the driver. Standard face depth of most drivers is 1⅝ inches. There are many variations, of course, with deeper faces and also shallow faces. The shallow-faced driver usually has a lower center of gravity and thus sends the ball at a higher angle. As a general rule, the deeper the driver face the longer the flight of the ball with the same loft angle. Many golfers choose the deeper-faced drivers because they like to see a lot of face and a lot of clubhead mass, which in their cases, leads to a feeling of latent power. My suggestion is that you try both kinds, deep-faced and shallow, and find the one that works best for you.

The "weighting of the clubhead" refers to the way added weight is put in the clubhead. Sometimes you will see a brass insert directly behind the sweet spot; sometimes heavy material, usually an epoxy, is inserted into the clubface itself to give foreweighting. The club with weight at the back will produce a higher trajectory than the club with foreweighting. It is another one of those decisions you should make after experimenting.

"Face progression" refers to the distance your clubface protrudes in front of the center line of your driver. That line can be behind the center line, too, in what is called an "offset" clubface. Bascially, the more "progression" or distance in front of the center line, the higher the launch angle will be. Offset drives hit the ball lower. If you are hitting the ball too high with your present driver, you might consider having your professional cut it down by shaving off some of the face.

The term "facing" refers to the radius on the club face from heel to toe. It helps the golfer to compensate for miss hit shots. It makes the player start the ball farther to the right on shots hit on the toe of the club, farther to the left on shots hit in the heel. The spin imparted to the ball then tends to bring the shot back to the fairway center. Ten inches is "standard radius" on a driver and that measurement is observed by most manufacturers.

The problem of radius is a complicated matter and one that you cannot do much about. We have to trust the manufacturers to produce the most efficient club designs, and they do. But, you need to be aware of all the factors that influence your decision on the proper driver for you, that "bomber" that carries your ball straight and far down the fairway. It may be a long search, but the result will be worth all the trouble.

THE PROPER SWING WEIGHT FOR YOU

Your club professional or any club repair shop can supply, at reasonable cost, strips of lead tape to determine whether you can handle a heavier distance-producing swing weight in your driver. I recommend that you experiment with your driver clubhead in this way. Put a 2-inch-long strip of the lead tape on the back of the club, above the sole plate and center it directly behind the hitting area spreading it from toe to heel. Hit about ten drives to determine how the change in weight feels. Then add more lead strips, one at a time, and go through the same procedure. When you start hitting most of your drives to the right, you will have the signal that the swing weight has become too heavy for you to get the club through.

Then, start removing the strips, again one at a time, until you find you can draw the ball with consistency. You'll have your answer in swing weight.

Some players shift the weight toward the heel or toe of the clubhead to encourage a draw or fade. Additional weight on the back of the head toward the heel will encourage a slice, toward the toe, a hook.

In the old days of the wooden shaft, the torque or twist in the shaft was so great, it was possible to rotate the head almost 90° by simply twisting while holding onto the grip.

SHAFT MATERIALS

In the early days golf shafts were made of hickory. Hickory was strong and flexible but was subject to torque, the force that causes the clubface to twist the shaft, particularly upon impact with the ball. Golfers in the days before the steel shafts were truly magicians in the way they could maneuver the clubhead on the ball in spite of the torque in the shaft. Nor was the torque consistently the same in hickory shafts. It was said that Tom Stewart, the old Scottish clubmaker, inspected several thousand different hickory shafts before he chose a matched set of them for Robert T. Jones in the 1920s. Incidentally, that set is on display in Far Hills, New Jersey, at the U.S.G.A. headquarters, while examples of very early wooden shaft club making can be seen at the World Golf Hall of Fame in Pinehurst, N.C.

When the steel shaft came into general use in the 1920s, the improvements in the problem of consistent response and lack of torque outmoded the hickory shaft overnight.

Clubmakers continued to seek new materials for the club-shaft, looking for lighter weight with strength so that the weight that could be removed from the shaft could be built into the clubhead with the result that more power could be delivered by the clubhead.

A few years ago, a clubshaft of graphite was brought to the marketplace by several manufacturers. It was lighter by several ounces than its counterpart in steel. But there were problems in the torque of the shaft; many golfers found that, while they might hit a graphite-shafted driver a greater distance than they would with a steel shaft, still, the direction was harder to control.

At a recent Long Driving contest conducted at Riviera Country Club in August, in conjunction with the PGA championship, Terry Forcum won using a white composition shaft that weighs even less than a graphite shaft. It is said that this shaft, quite flexible in its staff model, recovers at impact, squares up, and drives the ball farther and straight. Who knows? Perhaps there's a space age material down the road that weighs next to nothing, has no torque, has the proper flexibility, and will give us all three-hundred-yard drives with little effort. However, the fact still remains that steel is the most popular shaft material among long drivers.

GOLF BALLS

All officially sanctioned golf balls must meet design and initial velocity specifications laid down and enforced by the United States Golf Association. There are variations in the construction and compression of balls that will enable a golfer to pick up a few extra yards by using the ball that fits his swing.

Have you seen the ads on television or in magazines with the fellows running around in white lab coats and holding clipboards while measuring golf shots on a lined field? Their company claims by official test to have the longest ball. But so do several other companies. How can that be true? Is someone lying? Not necessarily. It's just that they are giving you selected test results, the conditions under which their ball comes out the best. This is controlled either by trajectory, club selection, velocity chosen, or wind conditions. For example, one ball may go farther with a #5 iron than another but not as far with a driver. Or it may go farther at medium velocity but not as far under high-velocity conditions.

What about the ads for "super balls" made by some firm you have never heard of at a post office box number? A company advertising in that manner is presently being investigated for false advertising. If such a ball were manufactured it would be in violation of the rules and its use certainly not within the spirit of the rules. Your distance, like your score, should be honest.

Basically, there are four different methods of manufacture at this time. The first is the solid ball of a mixture of durable synthetic rubber materials. The ball won't cut but, because it is hard to put spin on a solid ball, it is more difficult to stop on approach shots to greens. The second type is the two-piece ball with a solid synthetic core covered with Surlyn. This is a big seller because of its toughness and the longer distance it gets with irons. The third type is the wound ball with a thin balata

The ball has controlled the distance and therefore the game for hundreds of years. Shown here are the featherie (to 1848), the "guttie" (to 1902), the Haskell, and the present-day Haskell, a balata-covered, wound ball.

cover, a more rubbery material. The center of a ball is a small ball itself filled with a dense liquid wrapped with thousands of yards of thin rubber bands wound tightly around that center. The balata ball feels softer than the solid ball and it stays on the clubface longer, increasing the golfer's ability to spin the ball and thus control it better. Balata balls cut easily, so they are not favored by the higher handicap player who mis-hits them too frequently.

The fourth type of ball combines the Surlyn cover with a wound center like the balata. The result is a ball with more of the characteristics of a balata ball but with the cut-proof advantage of the Surlyn.

For most long hitters, the balata ball seems to go farther and, since it spins more, it is easier to control in the short game than the other kinds. That is why you will notice that the professionals play more balata balls.

The dimple pattern on the balls affects the way the ball is lifted in the air aerodynamically. Balls with large dimples will carry 10 percent farther with the wind because they will attain a higher trajectory. Balls with small, shallow dimples will bore into the wind better and carry 10 percent farther.

Most balls come in compression ratings of 80, 90, and 100. There are some made with lower ratings for driving ranges. According to some research data all of these balls will go approximately the same distance but will simply feel harder or softer to the player. My experience is that a harder ball will go a bit farther for the big hitter.

The average golfer will get more distance by fully compressing an 80 or 90 compression ball than he will in failing to compress fully a 100 compression ball. In cold weather it is often advisable to switch to a lower compression ball. Cold weather causes some loss of distance, but you will lose less distance with a lower compression ball.

I remember noticing on a cool day at the Masters a few years ago that the fine Connecticut golfer, Dick Siderowf, British Amateur Champion of 1976, was using a women's compression ball—and very well, too.

Just as you must find the driver that fits you, so too must you find the golf ball that works best for you. When you do, you might consider individualizing it.

For many years Dawson Taylor, my collaborator on the book, has played the balata 100 and 90 compression balls. He orders them specially imprinted with the key thought he wants to have in his mind when he drives. For example, pictured here are several examples of his clever idea. He also uses nothing but golf balls marked #7 because he feels very few other players use that

Dawson has his golf balls imprinted with special reminders about his swing. "TYT" stand for *take your time.* "See the number" means *keep your eye on the ball* and "accelerate" means *swing through the ball, not just to it.*

number and his chances of switching balls with another player are reduced. The ball imprint is a little psychological game, but there is no doubt that the positive thought is always a better one than the negative. If you get the chance you might try his idea to your own advantage and imprint the key thought that best induces your longest tee shots.

WHAT WE HAVE LEARNED FROM THE MECHANICAL DRIVING MACHINE

A number of years ago the golf equipment manufacturers realized it was becoming increasingly important that they have uniform, extremely precise testing devices so they could study and compare the design, durability, initial velocity, and various other flight characteristics of golf balls. Such testing equipment could be used to develop new and more efficient golf club designs as well, they believed. So, in a joint venture, they banded together and commissioned an engineering firm to build a number of identical mechanical golf ball driving machines. The cost was several million dollars but, in the end, each manufacturer and the United States Golf Association would have a similar machine for its use.

The results have been fruitful to say the least. Many benefits have resulted from the testing that has been done on these driving machines.

Tom Hardman is Wilson Sporting Goods Company's Manager of Golf Testing in Palm Beach Gardens, Florida. Every morning as I go to work I pass a yellow building on PGA Boulevard only a 5-par distance away from my offices nearby. I always look to see if the doors are open because when they are I can see an occasional lightning flash of white and watch a golf ball arc higher and higher in the sky and come to rest on a fairway that is marked off in 5-yard gridlike lines. A man in a golf cart hurries to spot the ball and marks the exact distance it traveled.

It is interesting, even exciting at times, to visit Tom Hardman and see the testing that is constantly being carried on. Tom is the

Note the "shaking hands" position of the club in the machine swing and how it models the position that we suggest for the human swing. This photo was taken with "Iron Byron" in action.

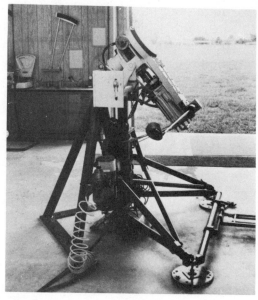

inventor of the dimple design called truncated cone, which the Wilson Company uses exclusively in its golf balls. One of the most important discoveries about golf balls has been the fact that altering the depth, the size, and the number of dimples can change the flight characteristics considerably. In the early days dimpling was done almost at random as the Scottish golf ball maker took a hand tool and struck the surface of the golf ball in order to roughen it. The earliest of golfers had found, probably by accident, that a golf ball that had been scratched in the brambles or marred by being struck badly a number of times went straighter than a smooth-sided golf ball that had no surface blemishes.

The mechanical driving machine that Tom Hardman uses is called "Iron Byron" because the classic swing of Byron Nelson was photographed and used as the model by the design engineers. Incidently, in the prime years of his game, Byron Nelson's backswing did not take the club to a position parallel with the ground, the 270-degree mark, but stopped at 265 degrees. So the machine's backswing stops at the 265-degree mark, which, by the way, is still about 20 degrees farther back than what the high-handicap player achieves. The machine works on a two-

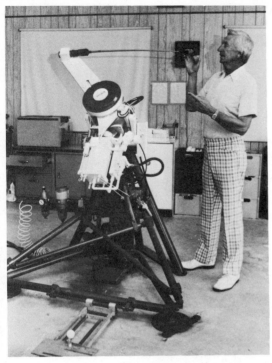

Wilson Sporting Goods
Technical Director Tom
Hardman quiets the
clubhead at the top
before "Iron Byron" lets
fly.

lever system similar to that of a human being. The clubhead is started at the top of the backswing from a fixed position at 5 degrees from parallel to the ground and the "arm" mechanism is connected so as to provide a double-lever action which delivers a "delayed-release hit" as the clubhead reaches the ball.

The machine works by various electrical and pneumatic machinery that can be adjusted to a range of clubhead speeds and adapted to different lengths of golf clubs. There is a large Plexiglas screen behind which Tom steps for protection every time he fires Iron Byron. Tom explains this by saying, "When we test golf clubs we hit the ball on several different spots on the clubface so we can tell the effectiveness of the design and where the sweet spot is. Sometimes when we hit the ball close to the hosel, we'll get a shank. You have no idea how startling it is to have that golf ball rattling around inside the building when you expected it to head out on the range."

Tom says we have uncovered many important facts about what happens when a golf clubhead strikes a golf ball at speeds of up to 170 miles an hour. With high-speed photography the ball can be seen flattening against the clubface and then springing back into shape and flying away at a tremendous initial velocity. By marking the ball with latitude and longitude lines, the spin rate of the ball can be determined with great accuracy. The spin rate has a great deal to do with the golfer's ability to control the ball. Hardman says the solid ball of today (of all makes) does not spin as much as the Surlyn two-piece ball and not nearly as fast as the softer balata covered ball.

Since Tom can be considered an expert on golf balls I asked him what advice he had for golfers in general about choosing a golf ball to fit their games. He said that, in his opinion, every-

Tom Hardman demonstrates the resilience of a golf ball with a compression-testing device. The compression of a ball is a rating that is more critical for the "feel" of a golf ball than it is for the distance it can be driven.

one should find the golf ball that suits his own "feel." "There is considerable difference between golf balls of different types and from manufacturer to 'manufacturer in the results of tests on Iron Byron. Some golf balls are not constructed under as rigid manufacturing standards as others. That's why sometimes you'll find one golf ball that differs considerably from the others in a given dozen. There's one popular golf ball I won't name that has a much larger dispersion factor than others. If you had ten successive identical drives with that brand of golf ball, you might find a twenty-yard variation in that ball from side to side and from the shortest to longest."

Tom went on to say that there have been great advances in club design in the last five or ten years. He says that there is no doubt that much of the low scoring of today can be attributed to improvements in equipment.

"One of the important discoveries we have made is that the ideal launch angle for a drive is about 9 degrees. We have found that drives at that angle carry farther and roll farther than at any other lesser or greater angle. This means that the average golfer should adjust his swing and club loft so that he gets the ball out on the 9-degree angle."

I asked Tom how he thought a golfer could measure his own launch angle. Tom said, "It's not too difficult, really. By using simple mathematics you can figure out that a ball launched at a 9-degree angle will reach a height of three feet at a distance of 20 feet, a height of six feet at 40 feet. You can stick a couple of poles in the ground at 20 feet or 40 feet and stretch a piece of string between them, three feet or six feet above the ground. Then drive your golf ball between the poles and have a companion observe whether your drives are going over or under the string. You can tell very quickly what adjustment, if any, you need in your swing or the loft of your clubface."

I asked Tom if the driver face angle should be 9 degrees in order to put the ball out at a 9-degree angle. He said, "Oddly enough, no. We find that the face angle needs to be about 12 degrees. This angle of the face traveling horizontal to the ground will produce the desired 9-degree launch angle." This, of course, varies with the player's angle of attack to the ball.

Also, players with extremely high clubhead velocities may need less clubface loft since they produce more ball spin which makes the ball climb to a higher apex in its trajectory.

Tom's advice to all golfers was, "Tell them to buy the best in up-to-date golf clubs. Be sure to get clubs that fit your swing, the right length, the right lie, the right thickness of grip, the right overall weight, the right swing-weight. Use a good golf ball with a feel you like. Hit the ball squarely on the face of the club. Then work on increasing clubhead speed by doing the exercises you recommend, Gary. There's no doubt that Iron Byron hits the ball much farther with his 120-mile-an-hour swing than he does with his 88-mile-an-hour swing!"

Arnold Palmer

"You do have to have a lot of natural ability to hit the ball 275 yards. This is something that takes a certain combination of reflexes, strength, coordination, and above-average timing."

5
DRIVING FOR DISTANCE

GREAT FEATS OF DISTANCE

What do you think is the longest drive in the golf record books? Was it made by Jack Nicklaus, Sam Snead, Jimmy Thomson, George Bayer? No, it was made by Kyle Wheelas of Beaumont, Texas. He once drove a ball that landed in the open cockpit of an airplane heading for Houston. When that ball came down it had traveled ninety miles.

No doubt that drive caused a great deal of talk at the nineteenth hole. Distance is inevitably the main topic of conversation when golfers talk about their efforts on the links. Commemorative monuments have been erected on the spots where great drives came to rest. Golf ball manufacturers constantly aim their advertising campaigns to appeal to your distance ego. Millions of words have been written in books and magazines about driving length and countless more have been spoken over the postmatch refreshments concerning one of golf's most fascinating phenomenon—distance. Here are a few stories about length that may give you something to shoot for.

Discounting Wheelas's "trick shot," there have been many other driving feats that must be placed in the prodigious category. Consider Mr. T. A. V. Haydon, an Englishman, who in 1934, while playing at the East Devon Club, accomplished the following driving feats in one day: (1) drove to the edge of the 9th green, 465 yards downhill; (2) overdrove the 11th hole, a 358-yard uphill dogleg; and (3) drove just short of the 17th, 450 yards downhill. Not bad for a single day's outing. Or how about his fellow countryman, W. Smithson, the professional from Sitwell Park who one year later drove the 416-yard second green from the championship tee? In comparison that may not seem so remarkable except that he carried a dyke which crosses the fairway at 380 yards from which the terrain of the hole runs steeply uphill to the green! (There was a following wind, but its velocity was not indicated.)

For these gargantuan drives, course and wind conditions have to be quite favorable. Most of the seemingly superhuman efforts had a bit of help from Mother Nature: dry hard fairways, a favorable wind, and in the two cases just mentioned, the smaller British 1.62-inch ball which travels farther.

A phenomenal driving feat performed in this country with the larger American ball was Nebraskan Bob Mitera's record hole-in-one. At the Omaha Miracle Hills Golf Course (what an appropriate name!) he aced the 10th hole, 444 yards distant! He was aided, however, by an estimated 50 mph wind gust, an October fairway hardened by a dry summer, and a downhill slope 290 yards from the tee. Even so, this was still a major feat for a guy who stands only 5'6" tall and weighs 165 pounds.

You may be thinking that you're not getting the distance from your woods that you should be. Under normal conditions the records show that even the big hitters are within a normal human being's firepower. Statistics compiled at a recent U.S. Open Championship revealed that the average distance of the drives on the opening and closing holes for the greatest golfers in the world was 244.3 yards. This compared with an average of 253.4 yards in a regular tour. Certainly the course, its conditioning and hazards, plays a definite part in those figures. The Augusta National Masters Course, for example, with its lush fairways, keeps the drive averages to about 250 yards. The regular PGA tour figures for week-to-week events show drives about 10 yards longer under normal conditions.

Another proof that 350-yard drives are not exactly common-place can be found in the case of a New York area driving range operator. His range measured 300 yards from the tees to the extent of his property. He offered a standing $5,000 wager to anyone who could drive a ball the length of his range in both directions within a given limit of time. He never had to pay.

Big drives that are made in the heat of competition seem really more significant because of the circumstances. Here the name players begin to appear, the ones that you have heard and read about. George Bayer, for example, had an actual measured drive of 420 yards in the Las Vegas Invitational in 1953. He had proof that it was that long because the ball struck a spectator and the distance was measured for use as future evidence in case of litigation.

But the men can't corner the market completely on driving records, for there have been a few women who also could sock the ball pretty well. The longest ace for women is a mind-boggling 393 yards made by Marie Robie of Woolaston, Massachusetts, at the Furnace Brook Golf Course in 1949. But for consistent distance, Mildred "Babe" Didrickson Zaharias took a back seat to few men and women in her era. Her length constantly amazed the golf spectators who were accustomed to seeing the ladylike pats of most women golfers. When Babe was asked how she could give the ball such a ride, she replied characteristically, "Why, kid, I just loosen my girdle and let her fly." Babe hit many a great tee shot in her career; but considering the circum-stances, one of her more unbelievable performances happened before she had even entertained the notion of entering the golf world. On the day after the Olympic Track and Field meet in 1932 in which Babe had competed in three events, she accompa-nied some sportswriters to a local course for her very first round of golf. With borrowed clubs she amazed her playing compan-ions by reaching in two shots the apron of the 523-yard 17th hole against the wind!

When Babe left the golfing scene, having succumbed to cancer, the long ball title was assumed without contention by lithe and strong Mickey Wright. Mickey once drove 10 yards past a 385-yard hole in Texas. Although she was aided by those two old helps—wind (40 mph) and that Texas hardpan—the performance still must rank as one of the all-time great feats for women. But Mickey has never been quite as long a driver as Babe was at her best, though Mickey was a good deal more accurate. She averaged between 225 and 235 yards on her drives, whereas Babe used to get them out 10' to 15 yards farther than that.

Great hitters have written their secrets on length, like Jimmy Thomson, the "King of Clout" in the 1930s. Thomson's instruction book, *Hit It a Mile,* documents the fact that Jimmy could really move it. In an official driving contest he averaged 324 yards for ten shots. In the 1935 U.S. Open at treacherous Oakmont, Jimmy was home with a drive and a 3 wood in two consecutive rounds on the 610-yard twelfth.

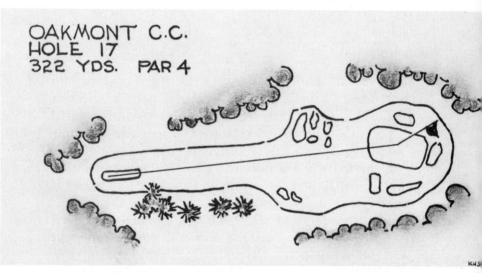

The famous 17th hole at Oakmont Country Club as it played in the "old days," before the tee was moved to the left. It was here that Jimmy Thomson drove the green but four-putted to lose the 1935 U.S. Open.

But Thomson was always amazed at the fact that when he went on tour of the United States to demonstrate his driving prowess in small towns from Keokuk, Iowa, to Butte, Montana, he would find unknown golfers, guys you never heard of, who could hit it farther than he could. No matter how long you are, there always seems to be somebody somewhere who can hit it a little farther.

One of the game's longest hitters of a few years back worked very hard to develop the strength in his left side until it was stronger than his right. His name was Clarence Gamber, a slugging sensation from Pontiac, Michigan. This 190 pound professional once entered a driving contest by walking to the tee in his sport coat and street shoes, borrowed a driver from someone standing by, and after being told where the farthest shot had been hit, promptly took one swing and out-flew the previous best effort by fifteen yards. He strode off saying, "Let them shoot at that for a while." Strength was also an important factor in the great driving ability of turn-of-the-century Englishman Ted Ray. Though his style was crude by modern terms, at a strong 220 pounds, he could throw a great deal of force into his efforts. He ably demonstrated this on one occasion while playing with three other great champions, all pretty fair country hitters—Harry Vardon, Alec Smith, and Johnny McDermott. On a 268-yard hole with an elevated green, the other three players hit drivers several yards short into the rain-soaked bank. Ray chose a cleek (the equivalent of our #1 iron) and carried the green ten feet from the flag!

But strength and size alone, as we have hinted, are not the only answers. The best example I know of is the case of a member of a prominent midwestern country club who had been a former Big Ten football player. At 6′5″ and 240 pounds you would think he could drive a golf ball across Lake Michigan, but he couldn't. In fact he could hardly hit it the length of the club's swimming pool. Naturally, this was a constant source of irritation to the big fellow. You can just imagine how he felt whenever he went out to play with someone new and they said, "Gee, a guy as big as you should be able to hit that little ball out of sight," and, of course, he couldn't do it.

The crowning blow to Mr. Big Ten's ego came after a disappointing nine-hole round when he dragged himself to the practice tee to try again to cure the anemic condition of his #1 wood. Try as he might, with every muscle quivering, he couldn't seriously threaten anything beyond the 200-yard marker. As he neared the bottom of his range bucket, he heard the solid crack of balls behind him and turned to see the District junior girls champ, all 115 pounds of her, flushing her drives out to a spot easily ten yards beyond his best efforts. That did it! He stomped off to the clubhouse, his ego irreparably damaged. He gave up golf and now has become a good gin rummy player. But there are some other, wiser choices he could have made and still happily be playing golf.

Flexibility is the least discussed factor influencing distance. Yet it obviously abounds in our younger golfers and is present as well in many of out longest adult hitters. One physically unimpressive young collegian who could really bomb the ball was little known Henry Fogg of Fresno State College. This thin, slope-shouldered young man only a little over six feet tall would stand no chance of being picked from a crowd as one of golf's longest—but he was. Although not particularly strong, he possessed fantastic flexibility and timing. His super late hit allowed him to accomplish feats regularly which few long hitters would even attempt. On the 11th hole at Pasatiempo on Santa Cruz, California, he regularly carried a barranca over 300 yards distant. In an N.C.A.A. meet in Eugene, Oregon, he topped his tee shot on the final hole, a 475 par five, then flew a #3 wood to the center of the green, a measured 315 yards. Henry Fogg demonstrated convincingly that size and strength aren't the only answers.

Louis Henry (Lou) Kretlow is six feet two inches tall and weighs 185 pounds. He was a successful pitcher for the Detroit Tigers and the Chicago White Sox. At the age of 38, Lou retired from baseball and entered the oil business. We all know that baseball pitchers are not supposed to be good hitters but Lou proved the old adage wrong, not on the baseball field but on the golf course. On March 15, 1961, Lou was playing golf in a friendly foursome at the Lake Hefner golf course just outside Oklahoma City. It was a windy day with gusts up to 35 miles an hour. At the 16th hole, Lou was driving with the wind on a 417-yard straightaway 4-par. The ground was normal, that is, neither unusually wet nor hard. Lou teed up a 100 compresssion

Titleist and, swinging a Wilson driver, gave that ball a tremendous smash. Lou *drove* the green but what's more, the ball ran through the front collar of the green between a couple of bunkers and rolled straight on and on and *into* the hole. Lou's longest hole-in-one record stood up only four years until Bob Mitera surpassed it with his ace of 447 yards in 1965. But Bob's was under more favorable conditions.

I talked to Lou not long ago and he told me that even today he continues to be a long driver at golf. As recently as the late 1970s, Lou won his local qualifying round in the Golf Digest Long Driving competition at Norman, Oklahoma, with a strong drive of 302 yards.

Talking about long driving, Lou claims that the golf swing and the baseball swing have many similarities. He says, "If a baseball player understands the golf swing, it can help him with his batting. In 1956 Mickey Mantle and the Yankees came into Kansas City. The Mick was in a bad slump. The first night he went without a hit in three times at bat. That evening after the game, we went out to dinner. We talked about the golf swing and I told him he needed to apply his golf fundamentals to his hitting, that is, to stay back of the ball or, as we say in baseball, not to stride too quickly into the ball. Mick went out the next night and got three hits. Later he went on to win the Triple Crown of batting for the year. The next time I saw him, Mick told me that our conversation about the golf swing was the turning point in his season. By understanding the golf swing, he helped himself in his hitting." If I am teaching a golfer who is tight, with an artificial-looking motion, I often suggest he simply make a horizontal baseball swing, and repeat the same swing with the body inclined for a golf shot.

The first hole at Cherry Hills in Denver, Colorado, is where one of golf's legends began. At the start of the final round of the 1960 U.S. Open Championship, Arnold Palmer stood seven strokes behind Mike Souchak, the third round leader. At that time the hole measured 346 yards and played straightaway.

It had a protective collar around the green, but in spite of it, Arnold, charged up in his well-known fashion, stepped to the tee, and smashed his drive all the way to the green, through the collar to a spot twenty feet beyond the flagstick. He did not sink his putt for the eagle 2 but his birdie 3 started him on the way to a 30 for the first nine, a 65 for the round, and an eventual score of 280 strokes which won the tournament by two strokes over Jack Nicklaus.

The hole is illustrated here as it appreared in 1960. In 1978 when another U.S. Open was held at Cherry Hills, the 1st tee was moved forty yards to the left and lengthened to 399 yards,

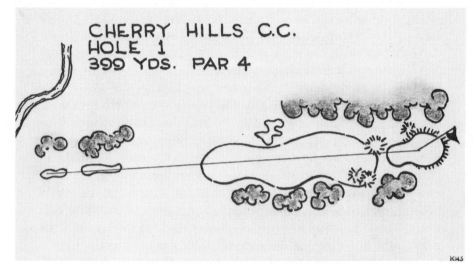

CHERRY HILLS C.C.
HOLE 1
399 YDS. PAR 4

KMS

The famous first hole at Cherry Hills Country Club, which Arnold Palmer drove on his way to victory in the 1960 U.S. Open

making the hole a moderate dogleg. Changing the hole created considerable adverse opinion and controversy. Today there is an historic marker near the location of the old tee commemorating this gutsy drive by Arnold Palmer.

I'd like to tell you about what I think was the most pressure-filled long drive in the history of golf. Imagine if you were in a long-driving contest and had to hit your drive 348 yards to win, and furthermore, you had just *one* ball to do it in?

That was the situation that confronted Evan "Big Cat" Williams in the third long-driving contest held at Pebble Beach in 1977. Evan was in his early 30s, slim, 6'6" tall, and weighing 205 pounds. He used a 44-inch, extra-stiff graphite shafted driver weighing 14½ ounces, 1½ ounces heavier than normal. His driver had 9 degrees loft. The final round for the $10,000 prize was actually worth $100,000 or more to "Big Cat" in driving exhibition money. One of the earlier contestants, Cotton Dunn, had already driven the ball 347½ yards, and it appeared that *he* would be the winner, especially since "Big Cat's" first four drives were errant or short. He was down to his last ball. One swing left—one that had to be perfect under tremendous pressure.

Evan himself tells how he did it in his book, *You Can Hit the Golf Ball Farther.* He says, "The preparation I had done for the contest had given me the confidence I could produce the longest drive so I didn't feel any pressure to do anything different. I had a technique I knew I could count on. I told myself to stay relaxed, take it back nice and slow, trust my swing. I took a few quick breaths. I find that taking a few short breaths sometimes is more relaxing than taking one deep breath. The oxygen opens a valve and lets the excess pressure escape. Anyway, it worked!" With Dunn's wife and daughter holding their hands over their eyes, Evan Williams hit his final shot 353 yards to become the national champion for the second straight year, thus securing his place in long-drive history.

HOW FAR DO THE PROFESSIONALS DRIVE THE BALL?

The PGA Tour keeps accurate statistics on many phases of the players' games. For the purposes of this book, the statistics on length of drives and accuracy (driving the ball in the fairway) are most interesting. According to statistics compiled through August 1983, Calvin Peete, one of the leading money-winners of the last few years, stood 153rd on the composite list of 168 PGA Tour players with an average drive of 246.5 yards. Accompanying Calvin as "short drivers" are such names as U.S. National Open Champions Hale Irwin (151st, averaging 247.5 yards), Lou Graham (154th, averaging 246.4 yards), and British Open

Champion Bill Rogers who stands 161st, averaging 245.3 yards.

Among the eight "long drivers" in this same analysis, with drives averaging 270 to 277 yards, the ordinary golf enthusiast would probably recognize only the names of Tom Weiskopf, Lou Hinkle, and Dan Pohl.

Another look at the PGA driving statistics brings out these facts. The longest driver as of August 21, 1983, was former long-driving champion, John McCormish, who was averaging 277.5 yards. But a look at the accuracy ratings showed John in 156th place out of 168 players, having hit only 55 percent of the fairways. Clearly long driving was not paying off for McCormish.

Jim Dent, another recognized long driver, was 91st on the accuracy list. Mark Calcaveccia, a newcomer, was fourth longest driver with a 272.9 average but stood 161st on the accuracy list, hitting only 54 percent of the fairways.

Getting to the heart of the matter, Raymond Floyd led the scoring records for the year with an average of 70.64 for 80 rounds. Calvin Peete was second with an average of 70.66. Floyd stands 51st on the long-driving list, averaging 260.7 yards.

So there is the odd situation of Calvin Peete being outhit by Raymond Floyd by 14 yards per tee shot and still able to run neck and neck with him in the scoring. Does this mean having the ability to hit long distances is not an advantage? Absolutely not. Possessing that extra power is a great advantage if it is used properly. For you very long hitters there is the advantage of being able to gear back, as Byron Nelson did over his entire career, thus being more accurate. It also means that being able to hit shorter irons to greens. Greens in regulation are highly correlated to good scoring.

The answer clearly is that we should strive to hit our drives as far as we can but with control that most of the time places them in the fairway. When we start getting uncontrolled distance, it is time to throttle back at a moderate sacrifice of distance. But for most of you readers, throttling back is not the problem. We're more concerned about adding distance so that you can putt for more birdies.

HOW TO PRACTICE DRIVING

I know you are serious about improving the length of your drive. I would like to suggest that you consider a regular routine of practice driving in order to incorporate into your swing permanently the fundamentals of practical, long, straight driving.

Of great importance are your tools. You have your favorite driver, we will assume. But you need the best possible practice balls as well. I recommend that you procure 36 golf balls of the same make that you are accustomed to using. It would be great, for this purpose, if you could afford all new balls but in the event that you cannot you should start to collect your slightly imperfect golf balls as you retire them from your game. Don't use any with serious cuts, though, as the results would be unsatisfactory.

You might consider buying three dozen "x-out" or "seconds" of the same make you use. In that way you will have an attractive functional group of practice golf balls.

Now, having assembled your practice balls, mark them distinctly so you can recognize them if you happen to drive them near other balls on a practice range. I recommend that you use a Pentel pen, which has an excellent, almost indelible ink. I mark my own practice balls on the ball equator, half-way around from the name imprint. And, for good measure, I put two more marks, always in the same place, one near the name and one opposite the name. This is a good practice for regular golf play, too. Your marking will be so individual you will never play someone else's ball. The dot marking can be recognized, too, from quite a distance away, and you can recognize your ball very easily when several balls are close together in the fairway.

I recommend, too, that you buy one of those pick-up-the-ball devices called *Bag-Shag*. The cost should be about $25.00. It will hold about fifty golf balls but is heavy to handle when it is filled with that many balls. Thirty-six, I find, is a comfortable number, and by the time you have hit 36 balls in succession, I feel you need the intermission to rest and contemplate your progress as you proceed to pick up the practice balls.

Now, you are heading for the practice tee. The ideal situation is to be able to practice almost with no distractions from other golfers. You should make every possible effort to arrange your practice time when there is nobody else to interfere with you. If this is not possible, try to get as far away from the commotion and noise of other golfers as you can.

Some people find that practice in the early morning is the most rewarding. The dew is sometimes a problem but the disadvantage of the wetness is offset by the advantages of being fresh physically and usually alone on the tee. Another good time is late in the evening. It will depend upon your work schedule. If you are a commuter in a major city perhaps a lunch-time session at a range or an indoor facility à la Japanese style is your answer.

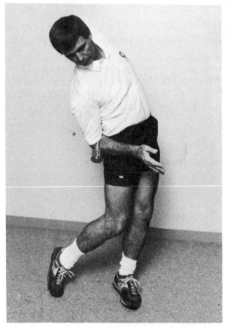

Do this swing and stretch exercise using the club across the lower back. Wind up as in the swing . . .

. . . then unwind. Repeat.

Put the club across your upper
back. The more deeply you
pull it the more it will stretch.
Do these gently at first to
prevent a pulled muscle.

Then turn back through, keeping
your head back for the full stretching
effect.

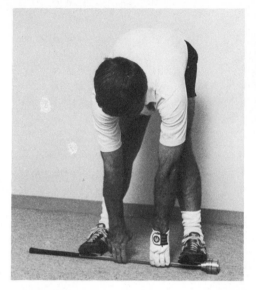

Place the club under the toes and gently straighten your legs at your knees. This will take practice, but you'll get better.

Hold the club between the thumb and index finger of each hand and extend it up and away from you behind your back. This is the toughest and most productive exercise in this series to loosen your shoulder girdle and upper back.

Before you start your serious driving practice you should go through the warm-up exercises shown here. I recommend them highly when you have arrived at the first tee without hitting practice balls. In fact, anytime you intend to make a serious full swing at a golf ball, you should warm up first. If you do not, you may run into serious muscle strain. Whenever you add speed to a physical task like lifting, throwing, swinging, etc., the risk of injury seriously increases without warmup.

When you are warmed up satisfactorily, and not until, you may begin your driving practice. Spill your golf balls about fifteen feet behind the area from which you will be driving. The idea of this is that you will be forced to take your time between shots by walking back to the pile and getting your next ball.

Throw down about ten tees nearby. You don't want to be running out of tees and chasing them, destroying your concentration. Pick out your target two hundred yards or more down the practice area.

If you are working primarily on first driving with control, put two clubs on the ground to represent a path to your target,

Visualizing a swing path to your target can help you produce the correct swing path.

which might be a tree or some other similar object far off in the distance. Also place one club that is parallel to your feet. But do not, and I cannot emphasize this point too strongly, do *not* make one swing without consciously aiming at a target or landing area. Golf is a target game. You are always aiming at that flag trying to hole out the shot or at some area to put it into a favorable position.

Now, proceed to drive your golf balls one after the other, all at the target. Take your time between shots. Stand behind the ball before each shot and visualize your line to the target. Then work on your body and clubface alignment by putting parallel clubs on the ground. This is critical, since long drives, with a good swing, that go in the wrong direction due to the misalignment will eventually require you to alter your swing and become less effective.

I happened to watch Jack Nicklaus practicing his driving recently under the watchful eye of veteran golf teacher, Gardner Dickinson, at Frenchman's Creek in North Palm Beach, Florida. Jack was working on his setup. On one occasion he stepped away from his ball three times to check his body alignment. Then he took a club and put it across his chest in line with his target to make certain his alignment was correct. If Jack can do this and feels he must do this, so can you.

As you practice, try to work on one segment of the swing at a time. Let's say you are trying to slow down your swing. You have been swinging too fast and losing control at the top of your swing. You might work on these two thoughts in succession as you make your swings. One time say to yourself, "slow back," even to the point of pronouncing "slooooooooow back" while you are in the act of taking the club away. One PGA professional uses the words "golf swing" to improve tempo. But he notes that the word golf is capitalized and spaced G-O-L-F to slow the backswing and "swing" is small letters and closer together to get speed in the forward motion.

Having driven your practice balls, check your results in this way. Walk out to the center of the area where the greatest number of balls are clustered. Count your paces as you go. Let's say that most of the balls are at the 200-yard range. You have a standard for the way you are driving today, one that you can compare to your results tomorrow or a month from now.

Check the pattern of your dispersal. How many drives went astray? Five? Ten? Was there a consistent error? More to the right than the left? All the facts about those practice balls should be registered in your memory so you can watch your progress toward improvement.

Where you can't hit your own practice balls but must use range balls, still note how things went during the session. Write down what is working. You can check your distance progress on the course when you play.

I believe in keeping track of my practices in the different aspects of the game. Many serious golfers keep diaries. I recommend that you keep one. You will be better able to see progress in achieving longer distance on your drives. It will give you a great deal of satisfaction to enter into your diary that today you were driving ten yards farther than you were when you first began your practice program.

WHY YOU MUST LEARN TO DRAW THE BALL FOR MORE DISTANCE

Recently *Golf Digest* magazine and the United States Golf Association conducted some interesting experiments with their mechanical driving machine. The experimenters were attempting to determine whether there was any substantial difference in the results of a golf swing that caused *fade,* left-to-right action on the ball in contrast to swings that caused *draw,* right-to-left action.

The tests proved that there are appreciable distance benefits drawing the ball and serious detriments in fading it. A controlled draw with a driver travels significantly farther than a fade.

The driving machine was set to produce a clubhead speed of 90 miles an hour, which is the speed of an average 5- to 10-handicap player. The clubface of the driver was adjusted 1½ degrees open for the fade, 1½ degrees closed for the draw. The two swings were identical in regard to attack angle and swing path.

The opening and closing of the clubface produced shots that traveled an average of 18 yards to the right or left of the center of the fairway. But the startling fact that emerged from these tests was that the lower flying draws rolled 16 or 17 yards farther after landing while the fades rolled less than 9 yards. The explanation for these results is that the faded shot is launched at a higher angle than the drawn shot. It has more backspin applied to it. There are also aerodynamic effects of "lift" and "drag" which are increased. The faded ball sails higher and curves to the right because of the initial clockwise spin imparted by the open clubface but it does not travel as far.

On the other hand, when the clubface is closed at impact the opposite happens. The loft of the club is decreased, the launch angle is lower, less backspin is created, and the forward speed is increased. While backspin is necessary to keep the ball in the air, apparently the effect of less backspin is more than offset by the increase in forward speed so the drawn ball carries farther.

Frank Thomas, USGA's technical director, explains that "the swing that produces a draw is more powerful than the swing that produces a slice." The draw swing approaches the ball from inside the target line on a more shallow and better angle.

The most powerful golf shots are struck from an inside approach to the ball.

Weak shots are hit from
an outside approach to
the ball.

The draw launches the ball with more forward speed and also promotes greater accuracy and more consistency. When the amateur golfer makes a slice swing, he usually does it by coming at the ball from outside the target line and at a steeper angle. The result is that the slicing action is increased, the loft and spin on the ball are increased, and the ball flies higher, shorter, and more to the right.

The tests showed that the faded ball averaged 207 yards in carry and ran 9 yards for a total of 216 yards. The drawn drives carried 217 yards and ran 16 more yards for a total of 233 yards. So the obvious conclusion is that with a choice of drawing or fading the ball, the ordinary golfer seeking increased distance should work to develop a controlled draw.

Incidentally, the test showed that the straight shot travels as far as the draw or even slightly farther. Although we will work to hit every drive perfectly straight, we should realize that if we don't hit it straight, we should favor the draw.

THE EFFECT OF COURSE CONDITIONS AND THE ELEMENTS

Bad-weather golf can be described as play in any weather that is abnormal. It might be golf in unusually cold temperatures, golf in strong winds, golf in the rain, golf in terrible heat. Whatever bad conditions you may encounter, you must be prepared to deal with them sensibly and if it is at all possible, overcome whatever obstacle is placed in your path. You may be required to play under unpleasant conditions, but you must always remember that your competitors must play under them, too. If you are better prepared than they, you will have a psychological edge on them. And, knowing that you have an advantage over them, you will play in a more relaxed fashion and probably win more often than you lose. But remember, unusual conditions can drastically alter your normal distance.

Let's examine a few of the circumstances that can be considered bad-weather golf and decide what preparations you should make in advance to deal with them.

At some time in your life, possibly many times depending upon the climate in your locality, you will be caught in a sudden rainstorm. You must always be prepared not only for rain but also for the sudden drop in temperature that often follows a storm. So, be sure you have a big golf umbrella with you at all times. A big one will give you the greatest protection from the elements. It should have a wooden or plastic handle, to lessen the possibility of your becoming the target of a bolt of lightning.

You should also consider carrying one of those lightweight nylon zippered windbreakers; if you play in club competitions where it is often necessary to continue to play in the rain, you certainly·should have a complete rainsuit. If you do buy a rain suit, it is wise to spend a few extra dollars and get a good one. The cheaper sets have an annoying habit of whistling or rubbing as you make your swing. So get a suit that is as quiet as possible because you do not want any unnecessary distraction as you swing. And of first order, make sure that it truly will keep you dry.

Now, let's talk a bit about the problem of playing in the rain and of playing in bad-weather gear. There is no question that the added clothing will hamper your swing somewhat. Your clubhead speed will be lessened. How much you will have to experiment and determine for yourself. Let's say that you normally hit a 5-iron 150 yards under dry, ideal conditions. Try some practice in the rain when you get your new rain suit. It is likely that the same 5-iron swing in the rain will travel only 140 yards. So, you have to build into your swing a 6 to 7 percent loss-of-distance factor. But, knowing that you customarily lose that much distance will help you choose the right club in the rain. You might decide that in general you need one club stronger than usual, so your thinking process might be "5-iron minus 1 equals 4-iron." A very important point about taking a stronger club than usual is that you do not, you *must* not ease up on the shot. Sometimes knowing that you have a stronger club causes you to hit it a little easier than normal. My advice is that you brainwash yourself completely and pretend you have your normal 5-iron. Just hit the 4-iron as if it is a 5-iron, and you'll be most surprised at your success.

When you play in the rain it is generally true that your best success lies in taking a stronger club than usual. This statement is not true, though, when you are coming out of heavy, wet rough. There you need to get the ball up quickly, even at the sacrifice of distance, so take a more lofted club than usual. Also tee your ball a little higher for extra carry on the drive.

When you are playing in the rain, the water gets between your clubface and the ball. You do not get the usual spin of the ball off the blade. So, you must allow for loss of spin in your judgment of distance. From good lies or very light rough, the ball will actually fly farther—that, of course, is the shot known as a *flier*.

It is useful to have waterproof shoes for your occasional bouts with rain or wet course conditions. Some of the rubberized golf shoes designed for wet weather can be uncomfortably hot on your feet. You may be faced with the dilemma of either having wet feet from water getting into regular shoes or hot feet from watertight shoes. Here, too, is another good reason for buying good golf equipment from the start. Cheap shoes are the first to leak, but even the best and most expensive shoes lose their waterproof ability as they age.

One of the most important bits of advice is: Keep your grips dry; if you can't hang onto the club, you can't take a good swing at the ball. Carry a dry towel draped on your umbrella struts for that purpose. Also carry extra gloves, so that you can switch from a wet glove to a dry one if you are forced to do so. There are some wet weather gloves now on the market that actually grip better when they are wet rather than dry. I always carry one for extreme conditions.

The best advice I can give you about playing in the rain is to take it easy. Try to swing with as perfect a rhythm as you can. It is very important that you hit the ball purely in the rain. So, if necessary, shorten your backswing and be sure to swing within yourself, which means don't overswing, don't try to overpower the shot or try to hit it harder just because you are losing distance on your shots. Let the additional distance come from using a stronger club rather than a stronger swing.

Try to swing with rhythm in the rain. You will be surprised at your success. It is especially satisfying to beat the elements. You can do it if you approach the problem and work with the rain rather than allow it to beat you.

Playing in wind poses different problems. In driving against the wind the ball should be kept as low as possible where it will be less exposed to the effect of the wind. When the wind is from behind, try to get the ball up higher than usual so the wind can exert a greater and longer effect in its flight.

To drive the ball in a lower trajectory, one way is to play it back farther than normal, toward the centerline between the feet. Try to have your hands ahead of the ball at impact. Since this movement of the ball placement backward and the hands forward may cause an open face at impact, it is most important that the clubface be turned slightly counterclockwise or "closed" to counteract these tendencies. How much correction you will need, you alone can tell by experimentation. Another method is to tee the ball normally but choke down on the drive slightly, widen your stance a bit, and make your swing more level rather than descending. You can practice this low-driving maneuver without any wind some day on the practice tee. I recommend that you do so. The ability to hit a low drive is a wonderful addition to your game. It will save many strokes.

With the wind behind, the suggested corrections should be reversed; that is, the ball should be teed a little farther to the left than normal and the hands should be allowed to be behind the ball at impact in order to produce a higher launch angle with more loft and, therefore, more carry. Stand tall, go to the end of the grip, and make a full swing, but not one with any more effect than normal.

CONSULT A PROFESSIONAL TEACHER

Since the early days of my first professional instructor, I have been an avid student of the game of golf. Many times when I have encountered minor problems with my golf swing I have consulted professional teachers who were usually able to spot my error and correct it. If you have not been taught by a professional teacher of golf thus far in your golf career I suggest that you seriously consider doing so. Furthermore, I have some advice on the kind of teacher you should select.

You will find, as I did, that no two golf teachers are alike. There are *talkers* who will talk the theory of golf to you and there are *doers*, professionals who will watch you hit a few balls and then suggest a minor change in your swing that may work miracles for you. On the other hand, you may experience a teacher who wants to make your swing over completely. You need to find a golf teacher who understands you, your personality, your character, your attitude toward the game of golf.

Many teachers are accused of making so many changes in a pupil's swing that the pupil becomes hopelessly confused and "can't hit a thing." This certainly may happen, especially if there are many faults to be corrected. All I can do is suggest that you be patient with your teacher and practice diligently the changes he suggests. Usually the results are good and if they are not the answer is, obviously, to seek out another teacher.

Once you have found a sympathetic and knowledgeable teacher, a person you like, confide in him. Tell him about your bad shots, the thoughts that went through your mind when you hit that crucial tee-shot out of bounds. Don't be impatient and demand instant results. Most of us have muscles that have moved in the same way all our lives. Suddenly we are told by the golf teacher that we must move a little differently. It will take time, maybe months, to change the habits of a lifetime.

Here's another good word of advice from someone who has experimented for years with the *best grip*. Don't fall in love with your grip. For some strange reason all of us seem to think that the way we first learned to grip the golf club is *the* way and the only way to do it. The slightest suggestion that a change of the thumb position or rotation of either hand one way or the other finds us fighting the change and perversely sneaking back to our first and *best* grip.

This is a serious matter, in my opinion, and one that should be clearly understood if you wish to become the long driver this book intends you to be. I have suggested many exercises for your entire body. I have especially emphasized the building of strength in your left hand, left arm, and left side. They will inevitably become stronger day by day. Therefore, you will find that it will take more and more power in your right hand to take over and pass your left hand as you swing through the ball.

Now, doesn't it make sense that if you are constantly gaining more strength in your left hand that the right hand will be more able to apply more and more power at impact without breaking down the left? It is true and the conclusion is that as you gain strength in your left side, you must be prepared to change your grip, make your left hand grip *weaker* (with a fractional counterclockwise turn and your right hand stronger with a fractional clockwise turn).

Here's another tip about choosing your golf teacher. Do not be surprised if you go from one instructor to another. Your first instructor may prove to be ideal for you and you would never think of changing for another. On the other hand, you may find that another teacher gives you an entirely different slant or approach to the game and your individual game, one that solves your golf problems. If so, by all means, stick with him or her as you progress in golf. But, don't be afraid to change teachers during your golf career!

I believe, too, that we should seek out those teachers of golf whose physical size and attributes are close to our own. The small player should not go to the tall, strong teacher for instruction; nor, on the other hand, should the tall, strong player seek counsel from a small, slight teacher.

If you are a woman, in my opinion, you should attempt to get instruction from one of the excellent teachers who is a member of the Ladies Professional Golf Association. I believe that a woman golfer will be more at ease with one of her own sex for a teacher. Some women golfers feel embarrassed when under instruction by a male teacher. So find that compatible woman professional who will teach you the game. She will know more about the proper club weight and swing-weight for your physical size and shape.

I recommend the practice of observing the great professional golfers in action. Nearly every section of the country is visited regularly these days by the Professional Golfers Tour. When there is an announcement of a coming PGA tour event near you, make every possible effort to attend. Be sure to go early enough to watch the players warming up on the practice tee.

When you go to a PGA tour event, go as a student with the intention of getting your money's worth in instruction from these great players. Many of the instructional ideas I have put into this book have come as a result of my observations of some great player using them and my adopting the idea itself into my game, then perfecting the idea to my profit—with the result that I gained a more perfect golf technique.

Sam Snead

"Strength is a factor in golf. You're building and then applying leverage with that club, and it comes from muscle power."

6
THE 350 CLUB—THE WORLD'S LONGEST HITTERS

In the early days on the PGA Tour, driving contests were a part of the weekly traveling show. They were all part of the hype for the coming event in those days before the advent of television, corporate sponsors, and tournament volunteer groups the size of Caesar's legions.

For a first prize of only $50 to $100, the players would take three cuts at the ball trying to keep one shot in play and hope that they didn't ruin their timing for the rest of the tournament. The longest hitters sorted themselves out pretty soon so that you usually knew that one of about three or four individuals would win. Over four decades the long-driving favorites were Jimmy Thomson, Chick Harbert, Mike Souchak, and George Bayer.

What the public didn't always see were the locals—the ex-ballplayer from the next county who could really move it, or the college kid who grew up in town as a junior golfer and now had a reputation for being amazingly long, or the huge local police officer who might have had a 16 handicap but when he got hold of a drive it was gone, out of the county. It's different today. The National Long Drive Competition has demonstrated that the longest hitters in the world aren't necessarily on the PGA Tour. In fact, most of them are not touring professionals. Of the winners over the past nine years, only one was on the tour, three of them were amateurs, and the others were nontouring golf professionals. From this event there has come more interest in long hitting competitions and subsequently the formation of a very select group of athletes who are members of "The 350 Club."

WINNERS OF THE NATIONAL LONG DRIVE COMPETITION

1975	*Geoff Long*	321 Yards	Butler National Golf Club
1976	*Evan Williams*	301 Yards	Congressional Country Club
1977	*Evan Williams*	353 Yards	Pebble Beach Golf Club
1978	*John McComish*	330 Yards	Oakmont Country Club
1979	*Andy Franks*	314 Yards	Oakland Hills Country Club
1980	*Scott DeCandia*	295 Yds. 18"	Oak Hill Country Club
1981	*Lon Hinkle*	338 Yds. 6"	Atlanta Athletic Club
1982	*Andy Franks*	346 Yds. 17½"	Southern Hills Country Club
1983*	*Terry Forcum*	307 Yards	Riviera Golf Club

*8,000 entrants in 1983 (a record). $45,987 was raised for the PGA Junior Golf Foundation. Over $300,000 has been raised for Junior Golf since the inception of the long drive finals.

The 350 Club is a collection of some of the world's longest hitters. The marketing brainchild of Mike Dunaway, golf promoter from Caesar's Palace, the Club boasts a team that includes four National Long Drive Champions, a World's Power Hitting Champion, the longest hitting senior, and the world's only "Golfing Gorilla."

The club's first event was the Slam-Am Pro-Am at the Sands Hotel in Las Vegas. Amateurs played with the long hitters in a scramble event. First, a long drive contest was held, and then a trick shot show and exhibition. Dunaway booked the group in Puerto Rico, Atlantic City, and Japan—and they were on their way. It was in Japan that Dunaway saw the hardest hit golf ball he'd ever seen.

The contest was proceeding under less than ideal conditions with a light rain falling. Dunaway led the competition by almost 30 yards with a smash of 358 yards when Tom Winrow stepped up for a final turn and launched one 387 yards. The announcer was speechless for almost two minutes.

The group now does package outings and appearances which include Pro-Ams, clinics, exhibitions and of course, driving contests. Dunaway sees a great opportunity for these veritable unknowns to turn into stars. He wants to change the slogan that now appears on the back of the 350 Club T-shirts, "Who Are Those Guys?" to "There Go the Biggest Hitters in the World."

Let's take a closer look to see what makes them the longest.

Mike Dunaway

The founder of the club is a 28-year-old scratch handicap player who stands six feet tall and weighs 226 pounds. He was a high school football and track athlete (discus) and attended the University of Central Arkansas on a football scholarship. Although he's only been playing golf seriously for nine years, he has managed to drive the ball 386 yards in competition and 486 unofficially on the golf course. Dunaway is strong, evidenced by a college 410 pound bench press and 1,500 pound leg press.

His training today stays clear of any arm and upper body development because of his considerable bulk there already. Dunaway does some running to keep his legs in shape but has a specialized program which he starts about six weeks prior to a long drive competition. He takes a Jerry Barber weighted driver which weighs 40–43 ounces and hits one hundred balls a day with it. Even with this heavy weight Dunaway can drive the ball 260–270 yards.

His technique emphasizes a left hand grip deep in the fingers, spot alignment, and staying behind the ball with the upper part of the body. He handles the tension in long driving by focusing on his routine and controlled breathing.

Dunaway's driver is probably the closest to standard of any of the serious long drive competitors. He uses a 43¼-inch dynamic X shaft, 9° loft, 10° bulge and roll, D3 Joe Powell headed driver. He's observed that in the long driving competitions, the shafts used by the winners are about one-third steel, one-third graphite, and one-third "White Lightning."

The reason the average players lose distance, in Dunaway's opinion, is that they start with a bad grip, poor alignment, and then end up at the top of their swing with too much weight on their left side (a reverse weight shift), giving them little punch to return to the ball.

Terry Forcum

The 1983 National Champion is a 6'5", 215-pound former rodeo Brahma bull rider. Now a golf professional in Ponca City, Oklahoma, at forty-one he is the oldest winner in the nine year history of the national long drive contest.

Terry has been playing golf for thirty-one years and is a scratch handicap golfer. He was a star athlete in high school, earning varsity letters in four sports. His longest drive in official competition is 369 yards, but unofficially, in an amazing feat, he drove the 547-yard 8th hole on the Lou Winston Golf Course. Recently, Terry hit a tee shot 429 yards on the first hole of the North River Yacht Club in Tuscaloosa, Alabama—and that was with no wind. Add to that a competition-measured 250-yard 7-iron at Atlantic City in 1982, and you get some idea of his power.

Terry has strong hands and forearms which he works on with a 15-pound weight tied to a rope. The rope is attached to a wooden handle that is then progressively rolled up by using both hands and arms in a forward extended position. He has worked on his legs with free weights, does Sit-ups regularly, but feels his flexibility is of prime importance. One exercise he uses is pictured below. He laces his fingers behind his back and has a partner force the elbows together and the arms upward to create more range of motion in the shoulder joints. I find this exercise better done while sitting in a chair. I also find that most people can't do it. If you are going to try, go easily at first.

In Terry's swing technique, he first picks a target at the end of the range, then starts the club with a low, slow takeaway, trying to keep his head perfectly still. He pulls with his left side but without feeling a lot of lateral movement. He attempts to delay the hit from the right side as long as possible. In addition, he says, "On slow motion film I've seen my head look at the ball so long that when my right shoulder hits my chin it looks like a punch from a boxer."

The bull riding probably helped him psychologically because Terry claims not to get nervous in an activity that leaves some of the best competitors with a noticeable tremor. He uses a strategy that is employed by at least two prominent Tour players, Lee

The "White Lightning" shaft was used by Terry Forcum to win the National Long Drive Championship.

Trevino and Fuzzy Zoeller—he talks with the crowd and gets them behind him. As Terry says, "They know who I am. This helps me to get fired up but in a relaxed way."

His driver is 45¾ inches long, D2 swing-weight, overall weight 11.4 ounces, with 8° loft, ½° open face, and a White Lightning shaft.

His advice to the average golfer is, "Develop a better body if you want to hit a better tee shot."

Victor Lahteine

Victor Lahteine has been playing golf for thirteen of his twenty-five years and has reached a handicap level of four. At 6′3″, 218 pounds, he creates a big swing arc with a full shoulder turn and long backswing. Active in sports until a knee injury sidelined him, he has driven 374 yards in competition and over 420 yards on the golf course.

He feels training is important and cites the fact that when he started working on a loading dock a few years ago, it helped him to get stronger and noticeably added distance to his drives. One exercise Victor does regularly is Sit-ups, but he wants to do more to build himself up.

Victor thinks his best results come from his natural swing, which is a bit cuppy-wristed in the left at the top. He's tried to flatten his wrists, which helped him hit straighter, but he lost distance so he has gone back to his natural position.

To handle the pressures of long drive competition he simply tries to stay relaxed and let his natural ability take over—he just lets it happen.

Victor's driver is 45½ inches long with an Aldila Boron 8 shaft, MacGregor M-85 deepface head, 9″ bulge and roll, and 9½° loft.

His conclusion after watching other players try unsuccessfully to hit longer tee shots: "They are too tense and too quick. Trying to hit hard makes you tight and short. They should loosen up a little more. Take a relaxed pace to the proper position if you want your best distance. Unfortunately, most people never learn good fundamentals; therefore, they rely on a golf bag full of compensations that just aren't conducive to long hitting."

Andy "Ball Park" Franks

This young man's story is an amazing example of dedication and work. At twenty-four years of age and already a two-time National Long Drive Champion, he defies the odds by only having played golf for 4½ years. A 5'11", 210-pound bundle of muscle, Andy Franks has not just worked on long ball hitting but also on playing the game. He is presently a solid scratch player and will try for his PGA Tour card next year.

Andy was a three-sport high school star in Florida but injured himself in his senior year in football. That turned him to golf. His longest official poke besides the two in the National finals was a 373-yard win in the Caribbean recently. He has driven several holes over 400 yards in length.

Although he has inherited a powerful body he has worked on the weights when training for football. Since then, his emphasis has been on losing some bulk across the chest and upper arms and working more on stretching plus running and bicycling for cardiovascular fitness.

Andy Franks has a straightforward approach to handling the pressures of long driving. "When you are the champ you are expected to do well. Everybody's shooting to knock you off. In that situation I do two things. One, I say, 'I know I can do it;' and two, I focus on good technique, the kind you'd use for hitting any good golf shots. I try to erase those other possible mental considerations— the crowd—the competition—from my mind."

One of the users of graphite shafts in the 350 Club, Andy has a 44-inch driver D3 with a 7° loft and 1° open face.

His recommendation is to work on developing better technique. "I go to my professional, Dave Ledbetter, for lessons twice a week. I don't try to hit it long there. But as my swing gets better, the ball goes farther." He adds, "I see too many fat, out of shape golfers who are being handicapped in distance and the whole game by their poor conditioning."

Tommy Mullinax

The "Mayor," as he is known by his fellow 350 Club members

because of the way he works the crowd like a politician, is a 36-year old PGA golf professional from Williamstown, South Carolina. He is 6'3", weighs 200 pounds, has a zero handicap, and has been playing golf twenty-four years.

Tom attended East Tennessee State University on a basketball and golf scholarship and also played baseball in high school. He claims not to be strong, but he is rangy with powerful hands which may have helped him to a 319-yard hole-in-one, driving the green on a 459 yard hole, and hitting 419 yards in a driving competition. His longest hit in recent official contests is an impressive 361 yards, 10 inches. His performance at clinics is of special interest because he can break par playing both right- and left-handed. Bob Rosburg says he's the finest striker of the ball of any trick shot performer he's ever seen.

Tom has relied mostly on his natural physical gifts, and started training on Nautilus equipment only last year. He feels it was of some help but the 35-mile trip to a facility caused him to be irregular in his workouts.

He hit his longest shots recently with a 46-inch driver, 5° loft, and a White Lightning shaft. His last two shafts were broken by other players, and so he's presently back to steel.

His approach to the pressures of long drive contests is casual but effective. In keeping with the strategies written about in the psychological literature on the subject, he attempts to minimize or put in perspective the importance of the task at hand. Tom applies this approach by saying to himself, "I ve got a good job; I don't have to win this thing. So just stay relaxed and enjoy it."

To the multitude of players he's seen who can't drive very far, his advice is: "Don't think so much of the twenty-five details in the swing you read in the last golf article. Getting confused means getting tense and tied up. Be more natural and you'll be more relaxed. That will be of some help."

Gary Hambright

Here's a relative newcomer to long driving circles who has great potential. At 6'2", 240 pounds, this 25-year-old powerful slugger has only been playing golf six years and has a three handicap. He played one year of college football and baseball after a good deal of success in high school sports including his high school home-run record. After college, in national softball competition, he hit an amazing 177 home runs in 110 games. This may be why he's been able to drive a 462-yard hole on the golf course and slam the ball an official 353 yards in competition.

Gary trains mostly to develop greater hand and leg strength. He increased his grip strength from a high school score of 95 to a present 145 by squeezing tennis balls and using a spring grip device. He believes that hand and finger strength is important if he is to maintain the club shaft angle for as late a release as possible. He also feels that he uses considerable lower body action, particularly a push off on the inside of the right leg. For leg training, he rides his bicycle and swims.

Handling the long drive pressure is not so tough anymore since he has toured two years giving clinics for the club manufacturer, Taylor Made. The experience has given him confidence, a critical element in trying to attain your top performance level. He works on tempo and uses Sam Snead's motto, "swing to a waltz beat," as an inspiration.

Gary has had to learn to try to draw the ball. "Some of the guys like Dunaway and Franks just hit it dead straight, but the rest get their longest with a little draw. I'm a natural fader which is pretty good for control but not as good for distance. The draw has also helped me to lower my trajectory and produce a ball that bores forward and runs farther."

Gary uses a metal-head driver. It's a 44-inch steel, dynamic X shaft tipped ½ inch, with a 9½° loft.

He suggests to players of lesser length, "Don't let tension cause you to pick the clubhead up too abruptly on the backswing. I like to use more of a sweeping takeaway. Picking the club up on the backswing encourages a downward glancing blow . . . and less distance."

Bobby Wilson

Like most of the 350 Club, this 27-year-old Texan is an athlete. He represented the United States as a member of the

National Team Handball group, a sport not widely known to the public but one requiring great stamina and good legs. A natural lefthander who plays from the right side, Bobby is a 6'3", 200-pound ex-college basketball player and scholarship golfer at Baylor who plays professionally to a zero handicap.

Bobby wears a double XL glove, a 14D shoe, and has an arm spread of over 6'7", which is almost five inches wider than he is tall. This is Wilson's advantage which he uses to its fullest by emphasizing a big wide arc.

In competition, this professional has hit a #3 iron 309 yards. He believes strongly in training. He owns a Total Gym which he works on at home; his emphasis is on the muscles of the back. Wilson found that heavy arm work, particularly push-ups, curls, and presses, tends to bulk his shoulders and chest too much, and actually reduces his distance production. In his mind, the importance of legs as a source of power in long driving is highly exaggerated. (Wilson can drive the ball 270 yards off his knees.) He emphasizes flexibility of the shoulder and back area.

For driving competition he feels that trying to be too accurate has hurt him by producing a little more tension in his swing. Bobby likes the term "free-wheeling" and would like that sensation to go along with his attempts to develop a smooth tempo and a clubhead that goes squarely back from the ball. He says,"I don't want to have to think about how I'm going to hit it. I've already done it thousands of times, and so I'd just like to get up there and let her go."

Bobby's competition long driver is the same one he uses for regular play, a 43¾-inch length, dynamic X shaft tipped ¾ inch, with a 9½° loft, 10° bulge and roll, in a persimmon, laminated head.

His advice to the seeker of distance is, "Work on your back muscles. They are vital. You should try to create a big arc with a good arm swing, and you need a healthy back to do that."

Tom Tuell

Baseball has a performing chicken in San Diego, and golf has a gorilla from Tacoma. The gorilla's human name is Tom Tuell.

Tuell, at 6'1" and 230 pounds, has a good start on the gorilla dimensions. What he actually does is give exhibitions in a gorilla costume, which is not as simple to do as it is to say.

First of all, Tuell can play. He's driven the ball 332 yards officially in contests and over the 410 mark on the course. He's a 33-year-old real estate investor and entrepreneur who has been playing golf for eighteen years and has reached a zero handicap. Tuell got the gorilla idea for golf from the great reception he received from people who were getting birthday greetings (a gorillagram) and a birthday banana from the gorilla-costumed Tuell. When other companies started doing wilder birthday stunts, Tuell dropped the unusual birthday greeting business, but kept the gorilla suit.

He started practicing in the uniform and found that although the costume was hot, cumbersome, and caused him to lose sight of the ball on his backswing, he could still drive the ball far enough to compete favorably in long drive contests.

Tuell qualified for the National Long Drive as the gorilla but was told he could only compete as Tom Tuell, not as his hairy friend. As Tuell says, "When I got to Tulsa, at the PGA for the Long Drive Nationals, it was the first time I'd competed as a human in four months."

Hitting in costume has taught Tuell to use visualization more effectively. Since he loses sight of the ball, he simply uses his brain to visualize its location. Another aid to Tuell has been to practice swinging a club through deep rough, which causes greater resistance. This is a drill he recommends to others for building strength.

Tuell uses a 46-inch metal wood driver with a double X tipped shaft for long driving, and a more standard club for normal play.

His basic advice to other players who seek more distance is "Work on improving your swing. Do it a little at a time. Don't try drastic changes that may destroy your enjoyment of the game and cause you to give up before you succeed. Most every player I've met has at least another ten yards in the tee shot that can come with better technique."

John McComish

The best player in the 350 Club is John McComish. At least that's what the statistics confirm since he is the only 350 Club member who is on the PGA Tour. Not coincidentally John was the PGA Tour's long driving champ in the statistics in 1983 with an average of 277.4 yards. But that accomplishment pales in comparison to some of his other long drive accomplishments. This 26-year-old, 6'6", 240-pound mountain of a man with a plus 2 handicap is a former National Long Drive Champion who, after winning in 1978, finished second in 1979 and fourth in 1980 and 1982. His longest poke in competition is 382 yards. One time on a 560-yard par 5 his drive stopped some 30 yards short of the putting surface.

McComish claims to be the physically weakest member of the 350 Club although he was a high school basketball athlete and college All-American golfer at Cal State Northridge.

In preparing for long drive competition John works to increase his shoulder turn for more power. After the long drive competition John says he must work to return to his shorter playing swing. In addition to the bigger shoulder turn he spreads his feet farther apart in the long drive and takes the club back a little more slowly. The reason he spreads his feet is to allow a wide enough base for an intentional extra body sway. He feels it's helpful in allowing him to create a wider arc, but it's not something he does when playing competitively.

John uses the same driver for play and long driving. It has a 44" length, 8° loft, dynamic X shaft, and a bulge and roll of 8°.

John watches a number of higher handicap Pro-Am partners and says, "A lot of people are not set up properly to hit the ball far. They have bad grips, bad aim and stance, and try to hit the ball hard on the backswing. Most people could hit the ball much farther if they made a better swing."

Tom Winrow

If there is any one competitor who is most feared, who (it is felt) can win on any occasion, the man who may be the longest in the world but has not fulfilled his potential in the National Long Drive Championship, it is Tom Winrow. This former high school basketball All-American who also played football and golf, stands an impressive 6'5" and weighs 260 pounds. At the age of 32 Tom, a golf professional, modestly professes to a handicap of "around 6," but he is much better than he claims to be. You'll recall earlier in this chapter that he produced the 387-yard smash in the rain that Mike Dunaway called "The hardest ball I've ever seen hit."

Tom is the only one in the 350 Club who doesn't train for long drive appearances, at least not physically. He tries to get ready mentally by simply picturing very clearly what he wants to do. He also recognizes that there is a timing factor in getting prepared and he doesn't want to peak early. In 1981 Tom won the only "power hitting contest" the 350 Club has held. The contestants hit shots with a driver, #3 wood, 1, 3, 5, 7, and 9 irons to vie for the title of all-around "National Power Champion." Tom was crowned the champion. An example of Winrow's awesome power is the fact that he hit his #3 wood 345 yards in that competition.

His equipment seems to fit his size. Winrow uses, both for playing and for long drive competition, a 46" driver with 5° of loft. He's kept the weight under 12 ounces, has a 10° bulge and roll, and a White Lightning shaft. One reason he believes the long driver is better for him is because he has short arms for his height. Tom believes that players like himself who emphasize lower body and good use of legs can handle the more flexible shaft, whereas those with a strong upper body like a shaft with less torque and less flex.

Tom gives the following advice to players who don't seem to get the distance they feel they deserve. "Work on the sequence of motion in the swing. Get your links firing in the right order. Too many men overuse their upper body and get out of synch. It's a continuous flow starting from below the waist."

What the 350 Club Can Tell You about Long Driving

Talking with top performers in any field always provides one with added insight. Such was the case in my conversations with these long hitting golfers. Let me summarize their advice:

- So much depends on proper grip, aim, and set-up.
- Developing a mechanically efficient golf swing is the most important element if you are to come close to your driving potential.
- Hitting a golf ball long distances is an athletic feat—you must have strength, flexibility, and technique.
- The draw or hooking shot is preferred for greater distance.
- Equipment is a matter of choice. The same clubs don't work for everybody, but players with a great deal of power do need extra-stiff shafts.
- Tension destroys speed. Do everything you can to stay loose.
- A relaxed, unhurried tempo in your takeaway for the ball will promote a good position at the top of the swing.
- Thinking positively will help promote the desired feeling of "free-wheeling."
- Training for golf will help you to hit the ball not only longer, but better, too.
- Although exceptional long hitting is a gift, everyone can learn to hit longer.

Dr. Gary Wiren

"I have never met a golfer who couldn't hit the ball farther if he were willing to improve his technique or physical condition."

7
RANDOM INSIGHTS AND SELECTED OBSERVATIONS

As we conclude this exploration of long driving there are a few loose ends to tie up, things that don't belong anywhere else that I wouldn't want you to miss. There is, to be expected, the traditional final exhortation: "You can be better than you are" by doing what is suggested in this book. That's okay because being better than we are at present is what it's all about.

It's not difficult to see how members of the 350 Club can hit it a long way. They, for the most part, are very large or power-

The principle of the late hit, technically called the conservation of angular momentum, is demonstrated here. You should have the sensation of retaining the loading action as long as possible before letting it fire.

fully built people. What about the smaller players? What do they have going for them? Ben Hogan drove very long for a 5'6" 147-pound player. But as a contemporary observed, "He had bigger hands and arms that I did at 40 pounds heavier." These physical attributes offsetting the stature limitations were accompanied by a technique that employed one of the longest delayed hit positions in history and an extremely wide extension at contact into the through swing.

Juan "Chi Chi" Rodriquez is but 5'5" and 138 pounds; however, only a handful of big hitters on the tour could stay up with him at his prime. He did not have big arms or hands, so

Swinging a driver shaft with no clubhead on it will help keep you light and quick. Such an exercise is important after a strength workout.

how does one explain his distance? Again a late release, more than average suppleness and range of motion, but more important, a nervous system that allowed his body to move quickly.

You could compare Rodriquez in golf to Ernie Banks in baseball. The former Chicago Cub hit a "ton of home runs" by seemingly flicking the bat and sending the ball out of the park. A contemporary of Banks was Ted Kluzewski of the Cincinnati Red Legs, who could literally sweep the ball out of the park with his awesome muscular power. Two different types of people, two styles, both effective. Kluzewski's equivalent in golf might well be George Bayer. At 6'6" and 240 pounds, George unquestionably was the longest-hitting professional golfer of all time.

Every era in modern golf has had a "king of the hill," one player who stood out above the rest when it came to long driving. But nobody dominated the field like George Bayer. He single-handedly eliminated the long-drive contests on tour because there was "no contest." If George was in the field everyone knew who was going to win.

His first year on tour, 1955, he finished first in 15 of 16 long-drive events. That is an amazing accomplishment considering that a player is given only three balls to hit and frequently doesn't get one in play. George was successful enough that after the first year he quit counting his wins.

Much of George Bayer's reputation as a big hitter was developed in the heat of tournament competition when long driving had to be accompanied by accurate driving if you were going to make a check. In a round with Jimmy Demaret and Porky Oliver he left them speechless as he drove the ball onto the green of the Del Rio Country Club's seventh hole, which was 436 yards long.

George was a varsity football and basketball player at the University of Washington in Seattle and also played semi-pro baseball. At that point in his life golf was more a hobby than a sport. Nonetheless, with his 6'6", 240-pound frame, he could power the ball out of sight. The driving-range operator at the university practice range one day requested that George stop hitting balls, for they were sailing over the fence, 275 yards distant. Bayer asked if he could hit some left-handed. After getting permission George proceeded to knock them out left-handed. He says he still can hit pretty well from the port side.

With George's size he developed a high swing arc which gave him great leverage. Add that to his athletic skill, flexibility, and strength and you can see why he was the greatest of the long hitters. He gripped the club from a natural arm-hang position and applied very light pressure so that he couldn't "choke off" his arm and hand speed. His suggestion to the majority of players with whom he plays in Pro-Ams is this: "Do some exercising to stay supple because you can't sit behind a desk all week and expect to come out and successfully perform an athletic feat like the golf swing."

Back to the small man for an interesting example. Steve Gaydos, now 73 years of age, was a little-known pro from tough Johnstown, Pennsylvania, coal miner stock. Gaydos was only 5'5" and weighed 135 pounds, yet imagine this: No takers appeared for his $10 bet that he could drive the 430-yard first hole at Sunnehanna Golf Club in Pennsylvania. He once hit a driver and 3-iron on a 560-yard uphill par 5 when the immortal long hitter Jimmy Thomson was short with two drivers, the second teed in the fairway. With such a small stature how could Gaydos hit it so far? Steve could chin himself by holding onto a bar with his two little fingers, an unheard of feat. Great flexibility, coupled with his abnormal strength, allowed him to accentuate the well-time delayed hit, which he employed to explode into the ball. Steve today recommends a golfer take some rail "to exercise with." When I asked him, "What do you mean by rail?" he replied, "Railroad track, cut up into pieces 4-8 inches long that you use to develop strong hands and forearms."

One of the current longer-hitting young players in the country is Davis Love III, a gifted collegiate golfer at the University of North Carolina. Love won the 1983 NCAA long-drive contest even though he doesn't stress long hitting and doesn't wish to be known as a long hitter. He *does* want to become a very good player. Love averages 300 yards for the driver, 275 yards for the 3-wood, and 250 yards for the 1-iron. That's right—*averages.*

He is not muscularly powerful and weighs about 165 pounds on a 6'3" frame. But he has developed an exceptionally wide arc on both sides of the ball and employs a move that every long hitter uses in his swing, the increased cocking of the wrists in the forward swing. In this move the angle formed by the left arm and club shaft actually decreases as the player starts the forward motion toward the ball. It's called by some *downcocking,* which in effect parallels the archery move of further drawing the bowstring for greater power.

Developing arc width on the takeway sets the feeling of width and expansion at contact.

Young Love developed this move by working on drills with his father, PGA professional Davis Love II, an excellent teacher. They worked very hard on developing the best possible technique; the distance came as a result. Father would make son hit drives 100, 150, and 200 yards while working only on form. When the form was perfected, Davis III could hit as hard as he wanted, providing he maintained his form.

Going back two generations, Chick Harbert won over 45 long-drive contests on the PGA Tour when that event was occasionally a part of weekly clinics at a tour stop. His psychological approach to the whole game contributed to his distance. He grew up on wide-open courses, learned to hit it hard, and tried to, most of his early career. His father, a golf professional, figured that when Chick got tired of tearing his pants climbing the fence to retrieve his shots he'd then learn control. When interviewed at an early Masters tournament, young Chick was asked by a reporter to describe his philosophy of playing golf. Harbert gave him a succinct answer: "To eliminate the second shot," was his confident reply. He played his early golf that way, with a freewheeling style that helped him to shoot both some of the lowest and some of the highest tournament scores in his era.

Harbert made "Ripley's Believe It or Not" by winning a driving contest at the Havana Invitational, where he launched one 358 surveyed yards. Second place Ed Furgol was 65 yards back. It's interesting that the stockily built Harbert claims the greatest length in his career was at a time he weighed 140 pounds. "There was nothing there to restrain the release," he said. Harbert believes his father, like Arnold Palmer's, was absolutely right in encouraging him to hit it hard early and learn to control it later.

Interestingly enough the player who took Harbert's place as the driving king on tour, Mike Souchak, reported the exact same distance for his longest drive in official competition, 358 yards. Souchak is the only golfer ever known to reach the famous 576-yard 13th hole at the Dunes Club in Myrtle Beach. He used a 2-iron for his tee shot and a driver for his second on the unusual dog leg to the right over the water. Mike adds an interesting note to the theory on drivers used for long hitting. He says, "My brother Frank was longer than I was. On the ninth hole at Oakmont he hit the green with a drive and a 7-iron, while the rest of the strong hitters were using two wood clubs and a pitching club. Frank used a 17-ounce driver. Compared to the lightweight drivers used by today's big hitters, that was a real war club."

Jim Dent was one of the first winners of the modern-day long drive contests. In 1974 at the Atlanta Country Club, Dent won the contest with a drive of 324 yards and 18 inches. He is 6 feet 2 inches tall and weighs 220 pounds. He uses a graphite-shafted driver 43½ inches long, weighing 13⅛ ounces with 12 degrees of loft. The swing weight of his driver is D-2. He claims that most of the time he swings at no more than 80 percent of his capacity. Jim claims that he likes to let the clubhead merely creep back from the ball in his takeaway. It's his only thought at address. "If you start too fast, you're dead," he says.

Dent gets a great deal of his power with strong leg action and also by the unusual trick of dragging his right foot toward the target on the downswing. He claims that he noticed Bill Casper making that move and admired Casper's control. Dent claims that the right foot dragging action encourages him to keep his upper body behind the ball and also allows him to make a proper shoulder turn. He also believes that it helps him to keep his head steady and reduces his tendency to sway. "If the head goes, the shot goes," says Dent. I agree with Dent on the steady head but I believe the dragging right foot action is too difficult for the average player to accomplish successfully. You might give it a try—who knows? If it works for Dent and Casper, it may work for you, too.

Jerry Pate, U.S. Open Champion of 1976, currently averages 257 yards off the tee, which classifies him as one of the middle-length long drivers on the professional tour. Jerry has an idea that some other good players use about getting that extra distance when you really need it. He says that he'll risk swinging beyond his normal limits sometimes when he feels a few extra yards might get him home on a 5-par in two or get him into a better position to attack a 4-par green.

Jerry will shift his weight a bit more than normal to the right on his backswing. He does this by extending the club back a little lower and slower so that he gets a fuller turn and longer swing. He will even move his head a few inches to the right, a move that is frequently labeled a sway. He claims that when he does move to the right it helps him to move aggressively to the left during his downswing.

Pate does point out the dangers inherent in such a sway, though, saying that on the downswing, "if you move your head too far to the left you'll block the shot to the right and if you don't shift your weight back to the left in time your hands may work through the shot and give you a hook."

I preach a more steady head all through the swing and putting all your power to work from a steady center. If you wish to experiment with a sway the way Jerry suggests, by all means do so. But be ready to abandon it if more erratic shots are not worth the extra distance you might get.

Perhaps the most impressive of all the long drivers in the world today is also a member of the 350 Club. I purposefully excluded him from that chapter because he is different and deserves special attention. Mike Austin is old enough to be a grandfather to most of the club, yet he still competes and is a sure bet to drill the ball past the 300-yard markers to open a 350 Club show. At a recent outing in Japan he averaged 318 yards for six balls, and that's at 74 years of age! Austin once toured 39 states offering $10,000 to any man who could outdrive him. There were no winners.

The Guinness Book of World Records lists Mike Austin as having driven 65 yards beyond the 450-yard hole at Wildwood Golf Course in Las Vegas which is an official 515 yards! That is documented. At age 71, he won the local qualifier for the National Long Drive Contest with a poke of 360 yards. Do you realize how far most 71-year-olds hit the ball? How does he do it?

Well, the first answer is technique. One of his fans says. "Mike Austin is classic in his swing. Such perfect flowing power, you can't see where he gets it. He'd make Gene Littler's swing look jerky." Austin is no average 74-year-old retiree, sitting in a lounge chair watching television, eating and drinking too much, and riding a cart every time he sets foot on a golf course. He is 6'1" and 205 pounds of physically fit human being who can nearly play to a zero handicap. He trains religiously, concentrating on Hatha Yoga and practicing a sound nutritional regime of eating vegetables, two above and two below the ground each day, fruits, fish, only occasional meat, and little milk or cheese products. As I write about him, Austin is preparing to play in the PGA National Seniors Tournament against men almost a quarter of a century younger. They may beat him, but they won't outdrive him.

WHAT SHOULD YOU DO?

Could it be any more obvious? To hit a golf ball a long way you must have something or some things going for you—strength, flexibility, body lever lengths, technique, or a good nervous system. If you are not blessed with one or more of these attributes, don't expect to win the local long-drive contest.

The promising message contained in this book is that, if you do wish to add distance to your shots, you can—providing you are willing to work.

While we have yet to find exercises or drills specific to golf for improvement of the nervous system, we know that traits like reaction time can be improved by training.

You have been given several strength development recommendations focused strictly on golf. Strength, particularly that related to golf motion, *is* a key factor in distance. We have also tried to impress upon you that flexibility is far more important than people think. Those who have strength need flexibility to create a full, freewheeling motion. Without it, strength is of little value. Good swing technique is probably the most important. But again, one needs a certain degree of strength and better-than-average flexibility to make a truly good golf swing. Your lever lengths cannot be changed; however, better technique can give you a wider arc, and a longer drive may provide more distance if you have a smooth, unhurried tempo.

Wild, reckless length is unproductive in the scoring column. But to have power and to be able to use it judiciously is a great advantage. For those of you in the majority who just want to reach some more par fours in two or hit middle and short irons rather than fairway woods, why not go for it? Make the effort. Start a program of improvement and enjoy the results.

Don't try to do it alone. If you have not been taught by a professional teacher of golf thus far in your career, I suggest that you seriously consider doing so. Find a professional that has the respect of his or her pupils and a busy lesson schedule, then make a commitment. Don't be impatient and demand instant

The trained eye of a PGA professional watching your swing can pick up the minor flaws that may be causing a power leak.

results. Most of us have golf muscles that have moved in the same way all our lives. Suddenly we are told by the professional that we must move a little differently if we want our desired result. It will take time, maybe months, to change the habits of a lifetime.

But know this: You *can* increase the distance you hit a golf ball. You simply have to know what to do and be willing to work. Now that you know what to do, the rest is up to you.

Maybe a better title for this concluding section would be, "What Are You Willing to Do?" Life is full of sermonizers who love to tell you what you should do. I'm interested in motivating not preaching. I'd simply like you to realize that you can be better and help you create the spark to do it. So decide how important greater distance would be toward playing better golf. If better golf is important to you, then allocate the time to get it done.

How far can you progress? Honestly, I don't know. No one, not even you, can predict that. But here are some clues. Remember, heredity is a factor. Our acquired nervous system, body proportion, innate strength, and flexibility all will place the eventual limitation on performance. Some people are naturally strong, flexible, or quick; others are not. However we all can be stronger, more flexible, and quicker than we are at this moment.

The answer for you may be primarily in swing technique. That's also where a player can sometimes get the quickest results. The right drill, suggestion, or analogy from your professional might add 15–20 yards instantly. If it's a technique change you are contemplating or working on, give yourself time to allow it to become a habit not just an idea. For example, developing additional wrist set on the downswing to create a more delayed hit in your link system, as opposed to casting your power away, is not instinctive. It takes time to feel it and a lot of successful shots to trust it.

Finally, recognize that long driving is an advantage only when it's effectively used. Golf is a game of numbers. A five with a slice will always beat a six by Tom Watson. There are odds to deal with and circumstances to consider when you are allowing yourself freewheeling reign. A player like Nicklaus, who was certainly one of the longest in his early Tour days, was smart enough to recognize that a fairway wood or iron from the tee of a par four or five was sometimes the better shot when you are considering the odds and playing for a living.

So, establish your priorities and goals, work hard toward their achievement, be patient with your progress, accept your limitations, and apply your new power judiciously.

INDEX